INTRODUCTION

The most important goal of this book is to offer Christians the needed scriptures and the outline for witnessing to unbelievers and leading them to a saving knowledge of salvation that is freely provided by the sacrificial death, burial, and resurrection of Jesus Christ, our Lord and Savior.

We are not alone in this ministry; we, being God's children, have received the Holy Spirit when we were born into God's family.

The Holy Spirit himself lives in us forever to teach us, to lead us, to empower us for service, and to reveal all the benefits that God the Father has made available to us through our position in Christ, which is our birthright and our inheritance that is promised to believers in the scriptures, we, being heirs of God and joint heirs with Jesus Christ, our Lord.

> For we have not received the spirit of bondage again to fear; but ye have received the Spirit of adoption, whereby we cry Abba Father. The Spirit itself [himself] beareth witness with our spirit, that we are the children of God: And if children, then heirs; heirs of God, and joint-heirs with Christ; if so be that we suffer with him, that we may be also glorified together. (Romans 8:15–17)

We only need one teacher, the Holy Spirit, revealing the scriptures and God's will to us.

> But the anointing which ye have received of him abideth in you, and ye need not that any man

teach you; but as the same anointing teacheth
you of all things, and is truth, and is no lie, even
as it (he) hath taught you, ye shall abide in him.
(1 John 2:27)

Being the heirs of God, his benefits are ours, and all of them
are received through faith and obedience to his word. Believe and
receive.

Having faith and claiming our benefits will set us free from
man's traditions that have been passed down to us through generations of hearsay and man-made false teaching.

Another goal of this book is to mention and explain a few of
those benefits by using God's Word for growth toward becoming like
Jesus as we walk with him in humbleness and obedience.

Bless the Lord o my soul and forget not all his
benefits. (Psalm 103:2)

My prayer is for you to enjoy this book and may God bless you
in your ministry and on your road to maturity in Christ.

SUGGESTED GUIDE FOR STUDYING THIS BOOK

To get the most benefit from God's Word and the teaching of this book, we have to make them personal to us. God's Word is written to and for individuals first and foremost, but was also written for instruction and to make known to us his desired structure for families, governments, and for the church, and how we are to respond to each institution in a manner that pleases him.

To feed and to grow and to make God's word personal, try putting your own name in the scriptures where you see the words *ye, we, you, your, us, brethren, thee, thou, saints,* and *brother*; unless in their context they are used otherwise. Most of the time, when the scriptures in the New Testament refer to people as they, them, their, and man, they are talking about the unsaved, the lost people, unbelievers, but not in all cases; so be careful and check the context in which they are used. Doing this will personalize God's word to you and give you joy, peace, and faith and will magnify God's love, mercy, and grace in your minds and hearts, plus making God's benefits real to you. So let us make God's word personal; you will be blessed as you do.

OUR PREPARATION FOR STUDYING GOD'S WORD

Talking to Nicodemus in the gospel of John, Jesus said:

> Verily, verily, I say unto thee, except a man be "born again", he cannot see the Kingdom Of God. (John 3:3)

> For the Kingdom of God is not meat and drink; but righteousness, peace, and joy in the Holy Ghost. For he that in these things serveth Christ is acceptable to God and approved of men. (Romans 14:17–18)

To be born again means that we have eternal life. What is eternal life, you may ask? We are told in John 17:3,

> And *this is eternal life, that they might know thee, the only true God, and Jesus Christ*, whom thou hast sent [emphasis mine].

So we can see that eternal life is a *personal relationship* with God the Father and with Jesus Christ, the Son.

Jesus said when talking about the parables concerning the kingdom of heaven in Matthew 13 and in the letters to the seven churches in the book of Revelation: "He that hath an ear to hear, let him hear."

Having an ear to hear means being humble, all sin confessed, and, by faith, ready for God's will to be revealed by the Holy Spirit so that we may be willing for him to work his will out in our lives no matter what he reveals to us, whether it is popular or not.

Here are some scriptures to energize you and to get you started in the right direction for this study of God's Word and for your journey toward maturity as you make them personal to you.

> As newborn babes, desire the sincere milk of the word, that ye may grow thereby. (1 Peter 2:2)

> Without faith it is impossible to please him: for he that cometh to God must believe that he is, and that he is a rewarder of them that diligently seek him. (Hebrews 11:6)

> So then faith cometh by hearing and hearing by the word of God. (Romans 10:17)

> Study to show thyself approved unto God, a workman that needeth not to be ashamed, rightly dividing the word of truth. (2 Timothy 2:15)

> For whatsoever things were written aforetime were written for our learning, that we through patience and comfort of the scriptures might have hope. (Romans 15:4)

> All scripture is given by inspiration of God and is profitable for doctrine, for reproof, for correction, for instruction in righteousness, that the man of God may be perfect, thoroughly furnished unto all good works. (2 Timothy 3:16–17)

BACKGROUND FOR THE PLAN OF SALVATION GUIDE

All mankind was lost, being born with sinful nature that we inherited through Adam and Eve's disobedience to God's command to them in the garden of Eden.

We are listing three accounts that show that all people are sinners by nature and by choice. Therefore, all are separated from God's fellowship.

First, we look at the Genesis account.

> And the Lord God commanded the man saying, of every tree of the garden thou mayest freely eat. But of the tree of the knowledge of good and evil, thou shall not eat of it: for in the day that thou eatest thereof thou shalt surely die. (Genesis 2:16–17)

Adam and Eve ate of the tree of the knowledge of good and evil, disobeying God's command. And that very day, they died spiritually, being separated from God and his fellowship.

> This one act of sin resulted in all of Adam's descendants to be born with a sinful nature, but God heard Adam's statement of faith that he made in Genesis 3:20: "And Adam called his wife's name Eve; because she was the mother of all living." And God responded to that faith in Genesis 3:21: "Unto Adam also and to his

wife did the Lord God make coats of skins, and clothed them."

Therefore, through faith and the shedding of blood to make Adam and Eve coats of skins [representing righteousness] they were restored and were once again able to enter into the presence of God for fellowship.

Second, let's look at Moses's account given in Hebrews.

> For when Moses had spoken every precept to all the people according to the law, he took the blood of calves and of goats, with water, and scarlet wool, and hyssop, and sprinkled both the book, and all the people, saying this is the blood of the testament which God hath enjoined unto you. Moreover he sprinkled with blood both the tabernacle, and all the vessels of the ministry. And almost all things are by the law purged with blood; and without the shedding of blood is no remission. (Hebrews 9:19–22)

Therefore, all sin must be paid for by the shedding of blood, which is exactly what Jesus did for all mankind when he suffered, bled, and died on the cross as told in Hebrews.

> But Christ being come an high priest of good things to come, by a greater and more perfect tabernacle, not made with hands, that is to say, not of this building; Neither by the blood of goats and calves, *but by his own blood* he entered in once into the holy place, *having obtained eternal redemption for us.* (Hebrews 9:11–12, emphasis mine)

Until Jesus's sacrifice on the cross, the Old Testament high priest offered up a sacrifice for his own sins and then one for the sins of the people on the day of atonement, and that was only once a year. These sacrifices did not pay for sin but only covered their sin for one year until the next day of atonement. But Jesus's sacrifice was much better than those of bulls and goats that were offered by the Aaronic priesthood. God's Word tells us about Jesus's better sacrifice in Hebrews.

> *But this man, after he had offered one sacrifice for sins for ever, sat down on the right hand of God;* From henceforth expecting till his enemies be made his footstool. *For by one offering he hath perfected for ever them that are sanctified.* (Hebrews 10:12–14, emphasis mine)

Even though all sins of all people for all time are already paid for by Jesus's sinless blood sacrifice, all people are born sinners as we will further see in Paul's account.

Third, Paul's account in the first three chapters of Romans shows us that the immoral man is lost, the moral man is lost, and that the Jews are lost.

> As it is written, there is none righteous, no not one: There is none that understandeth, there is none that seeketh after God. They are all gone out of the way, they are together become unprofitable; there is none that doeth good, no, not one. (Romans 3:10–12)

> For all have sinned, and come short of the glory of God. (Romans 3:23)

> Wherefore, as by one man [Adam] sin entered into the world, and death by sin; and so death passed upon all men, for that all have sinned. (Romans 5:12)

We have laid the foundation for our study of the plan of salvation guide in that the scriptures have declared that all mankind lost with the old Adam nature. Knowing that he or she is lost is really good news for the sinner because those are the only ones that Jesus saves. When he or she realizes that they can't be saved by working, going to church, and singing in the choir, keeping the Ten Commandments, being raised in a Christian home and can't get good enough on their own strength and determination to have a relationship with God, they are in exactly the right place to be saved. *Jesus is absolutely the only resort for salvation!*

In this outline, the plan of salvation guide, we have listed several points and the scriptures to support those points. These will be helpful in leading a lost person to a saving knowledge of Jesus Christ, our Lord and Savior. There are many more scriptures that could have been used to make these points, but we believe that these will be sufficient as you use them under the leadership of the Holy Spirit to accomplish God's purposes.

Please get familiar with each step and the scriptures in this outline and be ready to use them as opportunities arise. You will be blessed as you sow the seed of the gospel of Jesus Christ.

PLAN OF SALVATION GUIDE

Step 1: All are lost.

This is the necessary first step as we have shown previously by the Genesis account, Moses's account, and by Paul's account.

Step 2: God's will is for all mankind to be saved.

> The Lord is not slack concerning his promise, as some men count slackness; but is longsuffering to usward, *not willing that any should perish*, but that *all should come to repentance.* (2 Peter 3:9, emphasis mine)

> For this is good and acceptable in the sight of God our Savior; Who *will have all men to be saved*, and to come unto the knowledge of the truth. (1 Timothy 2:3–4, emphasis mine)

> For God so loved the world, that he gave his only begotten Son, that *whosoever believeth in him should not perish, but have everlasting life.* (John 3:16, emphasis mine)

> What is eternal life you may ask?

> And this is eternal life, that they might know thee the only true God, and Jesus Christ, whom thou hast sent. (John 17:3)

Step 3: Eternal life is a free gift.

Most people think that eternal life is a reward for a moral person (the goody-goody person), but we will see that it is a *free gift* for the ungodly in these scriptures.

> For the wages of sin is death; but the *gift of God is eternal life* through Jesus Christ our Lord. (Romans 6:23, emphasis mine)

> For by grace are ye saved through faith; and that not of yourselves; *it is the gift of God.* (Ephesians 2:8, emphasis mine)

> Therefore as by the offence of one [Adam], judgment came upon all men to condemnation; even so by the righteousness of one [Jesus] *the free gift* came upon *all men* unto justification of life. (Romans 5:18, emphasis mine)

Step 4: Jesus saves.

> For when we were yet without strength, in due time *Christ died for the ungodly.* (Romans 5:6, emphasis mine)

> For the son of man is come to *save that which was lost.* (Matthew 18:11, emphasis mine)

> When Jesus heard it he saith unto them, they that are whole have no need of the physician, but they that are sick: *I came not to call the righteous, but sinners to repentance.* (Mark 2:17, emphasis mine)

Neither is there salvation in any other: for there is no other name given among men, whereby we must be saved [the name Jesus]. (Acts 4:12)

Jesus saith unto him, *I am the way, the truth, and the life*: no man cometh unto the Father, but by me. (John 14:6, emphasis mine)

Step 5: Eternal life is for all mankind.

The next day John [the Baptist] seeth Jesus coming unto him, and saith, behold the Lamb of God, *which taketh away the sin of the world.* (John 1:29, emphasis mine)

And if any man hear my words, and believeth not, I judge him not: For I came not to judge the world, but *to save the world* [everybody]. (John 12:47, emphasis mine)

But now the righteousness of God without the law is manifested being witnessed by the law and the prophets; Even the righteousness of God which is by faith of Jesus Christ *unto all and upon all them that believe.* (Romans 3:21–22, emphasis mine)

My little children, these things I write unto you, that ye sin not. And if any man sin, we have an advocate with the Father, Jesus Christ the righteous: And he is the propitiation (proper sacrifice) for our sins: And not for ours only, but also *for the sins of the whole world.* (1 John 2:1–2, emphasis mine)

15

But we see Jesus, who was made a little lower than the angels for the suffering of death, crowned with glory and honor; that he by the grace of God should *taste death for every man.* (Hebrews 2:9, emphasis mine)

And all things are of God, who hath reconciled (put away all differences; namely all our sins) us to himself, by Jesus Christ, and hath given to us the ministry of reconciliation: To wit, that God was in Christ, reconciling *the world* unto himself, *not imputing their trespasses unto them;* and hath committed unto us (believers) the ministry of reconciliation. (2 Corinthians 5:18–19, emphasis mine)

God's Son, Jesus, paid the price for all sins, and the Father is not charging anyone's sins to their account for salvation purposes (*to be saved—born again*) all because of his love for mankind.

Step 6: Jesus traded places with us.

Jesus took our sin in *mercy*; not giving us what we deserved (spiritual death, the lake of fire, separation from God for all eternity).

Jesus gave us his righteousness in *grace*, giving us what we do not deserve—eternal life, plus all of God's benefits.

He *took* our sins, judgment, guilt, servitude to Satan, laws against us, our unrighteousness, and our blindness.

He *gave* us Eternal life, righteousness, the Holy Spirit, peace with God, a divine nature, access to God, and all things new.

Therefore *if any man be in Christ,* he is a new creature: old things are passed away; behold, *all things are become new.* (2 Corinthians 5:17, emphasis mine)

Step 7: Is all mankind then saved?

The short answer is yes. God, through Jesus's sacrificial death, burial, and resurrection, has already paid for all the sins of all people in the world for all times, past, present, and future, and has written all names in the Book of Life. *That does not do a person any good unless they believe that Jesus's sinless, righteous blood sacrifice paid for all their sins and set them free from the bondage of sin. Only through faith!*

> For *unto us(believers) was the gospel preached, as well as unto them: (unbelievers) but the word preached did not profit them, not being mixed with faith* in them that heard it. (Hebrews 4:2)

Forgiveness has to be believed to be received!

There is not going to be any more offering for sins ever! Look at these scriptures.

> For by one offering he has perfected for ever them that are sanctified. (Hebrews 10:14)

> But this man, after he had offered one sacrifice for sins for ever, sat down on the right hand of God. (Hebrews 10:12)

Jesus said on the cross, "*It is finished.*" And the sacrifice was completed (peace with God for all people for salvation purposes was obtained), *but it has to be believed.*

Step 8: All names are in the Book of Life.

Sounds too good to be true, doesn't it? But when we think clearly and truthfully, we will realize that any and everything that God does for us is too good to be true and that we don't deserve any of his blessings or his love for us.

This is a little known truth that is rarely taught or preached in today's churches. But wouldn't it be of great value to a lost person, for salvation purposes, as you're witnessing to them and exhorting them to trust the Lord Jesus Christ for salvation that they know their name is already in the Book of Life?

This may be a new doctrine for most of you, so let's see what God's Word says concerning the names in the Book of Life.

In Exodus 32, Moses had received the Ten Commandments, came down from Mt. Sanai, found the people dancing naked, worshipping a golden calf. He was very angry and broke the tablets of stone and had the Levites slay three thousand men.

The next day, Moses said to the Israelites, "You have sinned a great sin: but I will intercede to God on your behalf."

> And Moses returned unto the Lord, and said, oh, this people have sinned a great sin, and have made them gods of gold. Yet now, if thou wilt forgive their sin—; and if not, blot me, I pray thee, out of thy book which thou hast [already] written. And the Lord said unto Moses, *whosoever hath sinned against me, him will I blot out of my book* [not hath blotted out, but sometime in the future, will blot him out]. (Exodus 32:31–33, emphasis mine)

> He that overcometh, the same shall be clothed in white raiment; [signifying righteousness] *and I will not blot out his name out of the book of life*, but I will confess his name before my Father, and before his angels. (Revelation 3:5, emphasis mine)

> And I saw the dead, small and great, stand before God; and the books were opened; and another book was opened, which is the book of life: and the dead were judged out of those things which

were written in the books, according to their works. (Revelation 20:12)

And whosoever was not found written in the book of life was cast into the lake of fire [which is everlasting punishment]. (Revelation 20:15)

Some questions arise then: How can the Lord blot out the sinner's name out of the Book of Life if it is not already in there (Exodus 32:33)? Who is the overcomer who will not be blotted out of the book of life (Revelation 3:5)?

We get the answer to these questions from 1 John.

For whatsoever is born of God overcometh the world; and this is the victory that overcometh the world, *even our faith*. (1 John 5:4, emphasis mine)

What is the only thing that gets a name blotted out of the Book of Life? It is the opposite of faith, which is *unbelief*. The unbeliever will not be judged for sins for salvation but for their evil works to determine their degree of punishment in the lake of fire (at the great white throne judgment).

The believer will not be judged for sins but for works, good or bad, to determine rewards or loss (this being done at the judgment seat of Christ).

For we [true believers] must all appear before the judgment seat of Christ; that every one may receive the things done in his body, according to that he hath done, whether it be good or bad. (2 Corinthians 5:10)

Step 9: How do we get faith, eternal life, and all of God's benefits?

So then faith cometh by hearing, and hearing by the word of God. (Romans 10:17)

For by grace are ye saved through faith: and that not of yourselves: it is the gift of God. (Ephesians 2:8)

But without faith it is impossible to please him: for he that cometh to God must believe that he is, and that he is a rewarder of them that diligently seek him. (Hebrews 11:6)

Moreover brethren, I declare unto you the gospel which I preached unto you, which also ye have received and wherein ye stand: *By which also ye are saved*, if ye keep in memory what I preached unto you, unless ye have believed in vain. For I delivered unto you first of all that which I also received, how that Christ died for our sins according to the scriptures: and that he was buried, and that he rose again the third day according to the scriptures. (1 Corinthians 15:1–4, emphasis mine)

That if thou shalt confess with the mouth the Lord Jesus, and shalt believe in thine heart that God hath raised him from the dead, thou shalt be saved. For with the heart man believeth unto righteousness; and with the mouth confession is made unto salvation. (Romans 10:9–10)

For whosoever shall call upon the name of the Lord shall be saved [not maybe]. (Romans 10:13)

It is through faith and nothing else that we are saved. And faith in God's word concerning benefits is how we receive them also.

> For unto us [believers] was the gospel preached, as well as unto them [unbelievers]: but the word preached did not profit them, *not being mixed with faith* in them that heard it. (Hebrews 4:2)

Therefore, all that God has done for mankind, the paying for all sins (murders, lies, adultery, evil deeds, evil thoughts), and writing all names in the Book of Life, and not charging sins to anyone's account for salvation purposes doesn't do them any good unless they believe the gospel of God's free gift through Jesus Christ our Lord's sacrifice for them personally.

Step 10: Our ministry after being saved

We have believed the gospel, been born again, have received the Holy Spirit, been baptized into the body of Christ, and been translated into the kingdom of heaven.

> Who [God] hath delivered us from the power of darkness, [Satan's domain] and hath translated us into the kingdom of his dear Son. (Colossians 1:13)

After receiving all these benefits, we are equipped to be ambassadors for Christ and have been given a specific ministry to the lost, which is clearly stated in 2 Corinthians.

> And all things are of God, who hath reconciled us to himself by Jesus Christ, and hath given to us the ministry of reconciliation; to wit, that God was in Christ, *reconciling the world unto himself, not imputing their trespasses unto them*; and hath

committed unto us the word of reconciliation.
(11 Corinthians 5:18–19, emphasis mine)

More on this later.

As you have the opportunity to witness to the lost, this outline and these scriptures will be a big help if you use them as you are led by the Holy Spirit and for the glory of God.

May God bless you in carrying out this ministry is my prayer for you.

SOME DOCTRINES AND EXPLANATIONS

Sins are not imputed or charged to anyone's account for salvation purposes as stated in 2 Corinthians 5:19, where God's word says that reconciliation (which is putting away all sins against God) was done by Jesus Christ's sacrifice on the cross for the whole world's benefit and has given the ministry of reconciliation to each of us for winning the lost for Christ.

Notice that in 2 Corinthians 5:19, God's word uses the words *their* and *them* when *not imputing trespasses.* That denotes unsaved people. If he had meant saved people, he would have said our trespasses, thereby including himself as well as us, the saved.

Why not charge sins to their account? *Because the law has been fulfilled and blotted out.*

> And you being dead in your sins and the uncircumcision of your flesh, hath he quickened together with him,(Jesus) having forgiven you all trespasses: *Blotting out the handwriting of ordinances that was against us, which was contrary to us, and took it out of the way, nailing it to his cross.* (Colossians 2:13–14, emphasis mine)

For more to this point we look at the following scriptures:

> Wherefore, as by one man sin entered into the world, and death by sin; and so death passed upon all men, for that all have sinned: (For

23

until the law sin was in the world: but *sin is not imputed when there is no law*.) (Romans 5:12–13, emphasis mine)

For if they which are of the law be heirs, faith is made void, and the promise made of none effect: Because the law worketh wrath: *for where no law is, there is no transgression*. (Romans 4:14–15, emphasis mine)

For he is our peace, who made both one, and hath broken down the middle wall of partition between us; *Having abolished in his flesh the enmity, even the law of commandments contained in ordinances*; for to make in himself of twain one new man, so making peace; and that he might reconcile both unto God in one body [the church] by the cross, having slain the enmity thereby: And came and preached peace to you which were afar off [Gentiles], and to them that were nigh [Jews]. (Ephesians 2:14–17, emphasis mine)

Therefore *by the deeds of the law there shall no flesh be justified in his sight*: for by the law is the knowledge of sin. But now the righteousness of God without the law is manifested, being witnessed by the law and the prophets; *Even the righteousness of God which is by faith of Jesus Christ unto all and upon all them that believe*: for there is no difference: For all have sinned and come short of the glory of God. (Romans 3:20–23, emphasis mine)

For Christ is the end of the law for righteousness to every one that believeth. (Romans 10:4)

> Think not that I am come to destroy the law, or
> the prophets: I am not come to destroy, but to
> fulfil [do all that it requires]. (Matthew 5:17)

When a promise, agreement, contract, or a dispensation of the law is fulfilled, it is completed; it is ended. That is what Jesus did on the cross when he shed his righteous blood for all mankind's sins and declared, "*It is finished.*"

The question arises then: Why was the law given? We get the answer to this in the following scripture:

> *For if the inheritance be of the law, it is no more of
> promise*: but God gave it to Abraham by prom-
> ise. *Wherefore then serveth the law?* It was added
> because of transgressions, *till the seed should
> come to whom the promise was made*; and it was
> ordained by angels in the hand of a mediator.
> (Galatians 3:18–19, emphasis mine)

Who then is *the seed* that is coming?

> Now to Abraham and his seed were the promises
> made. He saith not, and to seeds, as of many:
> but as of one, *and to thy seed, which is Christ.*
> (Galatians 3:16, emphasis mine)

So we can see that the law was in effect only until Jesus came and fulfilled all its requirements: putting an end to the law and ushering in the age of grace, thus fulfilling the prophecy in Genesis.

> And I will put enmity between thee [Satan] and
> the woman, and between thy seed and her seed
> [Jesus]; it shall bruise thy head, and thou shall
> bruise his heel. (Genesis 3:15)

The battle was a massacre, no contest; Jesus's power was too much for Satan, and the victory is ours.

The law did not, could not, save mankind. All the law could do was to show man just how much he needed a Savior, who is Jesus the Christ. The very one Israel had been anticipating for 1,500 years but didn't receive him when he came.

> He was in the world, and the world was made by him, and the world knew him not. He came unto his own [Jews] and his own received him not: But as many as received him, to them gave he power to become the sons of God, even to them that believe on his name: which were born, not of blood, nor the will of the flesh, nor of the will of man, *but of God*. (John 1:10–13, emphasis mine)

SUMMARY OF NO IMPUTATION OF SINS FOR SALVATION PURPOSES

The law has been blotted out, and where there is no law, there are no sins to impute (charge to one's account) (Romans 5:13; 10:4).

In 2 Corinthians 5:19, God's word tells us that we have been given the ministry of reconciliation and that we are ambassadors.

> Now we are ambassadors for Christ, as though God did beseech you by us: We pray you in Christ's stead, be ye reconciled to God. For he hath made him to be sin for us, who knew no sin; *that we might be made the righteousness of God in him.* (2 Corinthians 5:20–21, emphasis mine)

Christians are to preach, teach, and witness to the lost, telling them that their sins are already paid for by Jesus's work on the cross—past, present, and future—*for salvation* and that their name is in the Book of Life and that no sins are being charged to their account (*only for salvation*, not for worship, fellowship, or for service); these sins have to be confessed for cleansing, to be righteous in God's eyes, and to enter into his presence for prayer and study.

> If we confess our sins, he is faithful and just to *forgive us our sins, and to cleanse us from all unrighteousness.* (1 John 1:9)

All of these wonderful benefits and free gifts are provided by God's love and by Jesus's sacrificial death, burial, and his resurrection on the third day, and the only way to receive these gifts is to believe that God did it for them personally through his undeserved love, mercy, and grace to them.

Too simple, you say? Too easy? There's no way these things can be true. The world stumbles at the simplicity of the gospel; it is foolishness to the unbelievers: the Jews required a sign, the Greeks sought after wisdom; both missed salvation by not believing the simple truth of Jesus's testimony concerning himself.

People of today are still stumbling at the gospel of Jesus Christ's finished work on the cross (only through faith, not works).

> But if our gospel be hid, it is hid to them that are lost: in whom *the god of this world (Satan) hath blinded the minds of them which believe not*, lest the light of the glorious gospel of Christ, who is the image of God, should shine unto them. (2 Corinthians 4:3–4, emphasis mine)

> I am the way, the truth, and the life: no man cometh to the Father, but by me [not a way, a truth, or a life]. (John 14:6)

There is only one way to come to God for salvation, and here are a few scriptures that describe that way.

> But to him that worketh not, but believeth on him that justifieth the ungodly, *his faith is counted for righteousness*. (Romans 4:5, emphasis mine)

> For *by grace are ye saved through faith*; and that not of yourselves: it is the gift of God. Not of works, lest any man should boast. (Ephesians 2:8–9, emphasis mine)

For what saith the scriptures? *Abraham believed
God, and it was counted unto him for righteousness.*
(Romans 4:3, emphasis mine)

And being fully persuaded that what he had
promised, he was able to perform. And therefore
it was imputed to him for righteousness. Now
it was not written for his sake alone, that it was
imputed to him; *But for us (you) also to whom it
shall be imputed, if we believe on him* that raised
up Jesus our Lord from the dead: Who was delivered for our offences, and was raised again for our
justification. (Romans 4:21–25, emphasis mine)

God's mercy equals no imputation of sins for salvation because
Jesus paid for all the sins of the whole world.

God's grace equals imputation of righteousness to all true believers' account.

For he hath made him to be sin for us, who knew
no sin: that *we might be made the righteousness of
God in him.* (2 Corinthians 5:21, emphasis mine)

For by one offering he hath perfected for ever
them that are sanctified [believers]. (Hebrews
10:14)

We are sent by whom? And how are we sent?

We already have a ministry of reconciliation and are ambassadors. Now we want to know who it is that sends us on our mission to
the world and our main purpose in this life.

Jesus tells us when praying to the Father in John 17:18,

As thou hast sent me into the world, even so have
I also sent them into the world.

We know that Jesus was talking with his disciples and was talking about their ministry, *but he included us* as we see in John 17:20,

> Neither pray I for these alone, but for them also
> which shall believe on me through their word.

If you are a believer, that verse included you and all other true believers.

Okay, we know that Jesus sends us, and he sends us as he was sent, so how was Jesus sent? We go to the scriptures to find the answers to all our questions by asking, seeking, and knocking as stated in the following scripture:

> Ask, and it shall be given you; seek, and you will
> find; knock, and it shall be opened unto you.
> For every one that asketh receiveth; and he that
> seeketh findeth; and to him that knocketh it shall
> be opened [not maybe]. (Matthew 7:7–8)

Those verses show us that it is by prayer, study, and by consistently believing God's word that we will find his will for us, which is our answer.

Hebrews 10:1–4 talks about the blood of bulls and goats not being possible to take away sins forever but talking about Jesus's blood.

> Wherefore when he cometh into the world, he
> saith, sacrifice and offering thou wouldest not,
> but a body hast thou prepared me: in burnt offer-
> ings and sacrifices for sin thou hast had no plea-
> sure. Then said I, lo, I come (in the volume of the
> book it is written of me) to do thy will, o God.
> (Hebrews 10:5–7)

I can of mine own self do nothing: as I hear, I
judge: and my judgment is just; because *I seek not
my own will, but the will of the Father which hath
sent me.* (John 5:30, emphasis mine)

For *I came down from heaven, not to do mine own
will, but the will of him that sent me.* (John 6:38,
emphasis mine)

And he that sent me is with me; the Father hath
not left me alone; *for I do always those things that
please him.* (John 8:29, emphasis mine)

We can see that Jesus's life mission was to do the will of the
Father who sent him. (see John 17:18) Therefore, we are sent to do
the Father's will in all things, just as Jesus was sent. We do the will of
the Father and fulfill the law as Jesus did when we humble ourselves,
walk in the Spirit, abide in Christ, loving God and others.

For all the law is fulfilled in one word, even in
this; Thou shalt love thy neighbor as thyself.
(Galatians 5:14)

Jesus had presented himself to the Jews as the Messiah, the king
that they were looking for, but they rejected him as a nation. Then
he began calling to himself personal disciplines as we see in the following scripture:

Come unto me, all ye that labour and are heavy
laden, and I will give you rest. (Matthew 11:28)

This call was for sinners to come and be saved (be born again).
This was also for all individuals to take advantage of the "*peace with
God*" that was purchased by Christ on the cross for all mankind, but

Jesus didn't stop there; he also had another rest in mind that we will see in the following scripture:

> Take my yoke upon you, learn of me; for I am meek and lowly in heart: and *ye shall find rest unto your souls*. For my yoke is easy, and my burden is light. (Matthew 11:29–30, emphasis mine)

Jesus said take *my yoke* (doing the will of the Father), not our yoke (our will), and learn of me by studying, listening to the Holy Spirit's teaching, asking, seeking, and by knocking, and by prayer.

This "soul rest" is to have the *peace of God* so that we might be able to worship, have fellowship, and for our service, and to have a clear conscience in the presence of God.

> Verse 29—for being born into the family of God; "*peace with God*"
>
> Verse 30—for the "*peace of God*"; for soul rest, the abundant life, and spiritual growth toward being like Christ

Soul rest is the one thing that all mankind yearns for whether they know it or not, and it is freely given through faith and obedience to God's word.

We have been given authority by Jesus, an ambassadorship, a message of reconciliation, and a purpose, which is to do the will of God. We are fully equipped for our new life of service and challenged to do what this scripture says:

> And whatsoever ye do in word or deed, do all in the name of the Lord Jesus, giving thanks to God and the Father by him. (Colossians 3:17)

God's will is our goal and calling, doing as Jesus, our example, always did.

SOME BENEFITS AND ENABLEMENT

We are authorized, equipped, and sent. Where does our power and direction come from to accomplish God's will? We need to look back in the Old Testament to see how the prophets and God's men got their power and direction for their mighty missions to fulfil the will of God.

Moses is one example for us. God was speaking to Moses out of the burning bush and said this:

> Now, therefore, behold, the cry of the children of Israel is come unto me; and I have also seen the oppression wherewith the Egyptians oppress them. Come now, therefore, and I will send thee unto Pharaoh, that thou mayest bring forth my people the children of Israel out of Egypt. And Moses said unto God, who am I, that I should go unto pharaoh, and that I should bring forth the children of Israel out of Egypt? And he said *certainly I will be with thee.* (Exodus 3:9–12, emphasis mine)

Joshua is another example. When Israel was preparing to cross the Jordan river at Kadesh-Barnea to go into the promised land (Canaan), God told Joshua in the following:

> And the Lord said unto Joshua, this day will I begin to magnify thee in the sight of all Israel,

that they may know that *as I was with Moses, so I will be with thee.* (Joshua 3:7)

Gideon was hiding from the Midianites by the winepress, threshing his wheat, and the Lord appeared to him, and these were his words:

And the Angel of the Lord appeared unto him, and said unto him, *the Lord is with thee*, thou mighty man of valor, And the Lord looked upon him, and said, go in this thy might, and thou shalt save Israel from the hand of the Midianites; *have I not sent thee?* And the Lord said unto him surely *I will be with thee*, and thou shalt smite the Midianites as one man. (Judges 6:12,14,16, emphasis mine)

The common thread among them was that almighty God "was with them," and they could not be defeated when they were obedient to him. Knowing that God was with them gave them the assurance, strength, and the courage for them to step out on faith and allow God to accomplish his mission through their trust in his word to them.

Wouldn't it be wonderful if we had the same confidence that they had concerning God's promise to be with us and the power to accomplish our God-given missions as ambassadors for Christ in this world?

Well, we have some great news for you friends: We are more equipped and more blessed than Moses, Joshua, or Gideon, or any other people who have ever lived because God is not only with us; "he is in us." We are his tabernacle: He, God the Father, God the Son, and God the Holy Spirit make their home in us!

That great news is hard to believe, isn't it? Would you believe it if God's word says that it is true? Look at and believe these scriptures.

Know ye not that ye are the temple of God and that the Spirit of God dwelleth in you? (1 Corinthians 3:16)

For in him [Jesus] dwelleth all the fulness of the
Godhead bodily [God the Father, God the Son,
and God the Holy Spirit]. And ye are complete
in him which is the head of all principality and
power. (Colossians 2:9–10)

And because ye are sons, God sent forth the Spirit
of his Son into your hearts, crying Abba, Father.
(Galatians 4:6)

My little children, of whom I travail in birth again
until Christ be formed in you. (Galatians 4:19)

Believe me that I am in the Father, and the Father
in me; or believe me for the very works' sake [if
we have Jesus, we have the Father also]. (John
14:11)

And what agreement hath the temple of God
with idols? For ye [put your name here] are the
temple of the living God; as God hath said, I will
dwell in them and walk in them; and I will be their
God, and they shall be my people. (2 Corinthians
6:16, emphasis mine)

No man hath seen God at any time. If we love
one another, God dwelleth in us, and his love is
perfected in us. Hereby know we that we dwell in
him, and he in us, because he hath given us of his
Spirit. (1 John 4:12–13, emphasis mine)

The Apostle Paul is revealing a mystery given to him to give to
us and says,

Even the mystery which hath been hid from ages
and from generations, but now is made manifest

to his saints: To whom God would make known what is the riches of his glory of his mystery among the Gentiles; which is *Christ in you*, the hope of glory. (Colossians 1 26–27, emphasis mine)

I am crucified with Christ; nevertheless I live; *yet not I*, but *Christ liveth in me*: and the life which I now live in the flesh I live by the faith of the Son of God, who loved me, and gave himself for me. (Galatians 2:20, emphasis mine)

For ye are dead, and *your life is hid with Christ in God*. (Colossians 3:3, emphasis mine)

That they [believers] all may be one, as thou, Father, art in me, *and I in thee, that they also may be one in us*: that the world may believe that thou hast sent me. *I in them, and thou in me, that they may be made perfect in one*; and that the world may know that thou hast sent me, and hast loved them as thou hast loved me. (John 17:21–23, emphasis mine)

What? Know ye not that your body is the temple of the Holy Spirit which is in you, which ye have of God, and ye are not your own? For ye are bought with a price; therefore glorify God in your body and in your spirit, which are God's. (1 Corinthians 6:19–20, emphasis mine)

And when he was demanded of the Pharisees, when the kingdom of God should come, he answered them and said, The kingdom of God cometh not with observation: Neither shall they say, lo here! Or, lo there! For behold, *the kingdom of God is within you.* (Luke 17:20–21, emphasis mine)

For the kingdom of God is not meat and drink; but *righteousness, and peace, and joy in the Holy Ghost.* For he that in these things serveth Christ is acceptable to God, and approved of men. (Romans 14:17–18, emphasis mine)

In Philippians 2, Paul tells us to work out our own salvation with fear and trembling (showing Jesus to the world). Why?

For *it is God which worketh in you* both the will and to do of his good pleasure. (Philippians 2:13, emphasis mine)

There is one body, and one Spirit, even as ye are called in one hope of your calling; one Lord, one faith, one baptism, one God and Father of all, who is above all, and through all, and *in you all.* (Ephesians 4:4–6, emphasis mine)

You can see that we are more blessed than the Old Testament prophets because we have a much better and closer relationship with God than them, by him being *in us* as opposed to his being *with them* (Moses, Joshua, and Gideon).

We are baptized into the body of Christ; he is the head, and we are his body. Also, we're married to Christ; we, the church, are his bride.

Wherefore, my brethren, *ye also are become dead to the law by the body of Christ; that ye should be married to another, even to him [Jesus] who is raised from the dead, that we should bring forth fruit unto God.* (Romans 7:4, emphasis mine)

A man or woman is much closer and more intimate with their spouse, more so than with their dad, mom, brother, sister, or even their children. Just like our relationship with Christ, we are *one with him* as a man and woman are one by marriage.

The marriage of the natural man and woman is ended by the death of either party, but our marriage to Jesus is a spiritual one and will last forever. What a comfort and what a blessing!

The Old Testament prophets could see the suffering servant and also the king on the throne, but they could not see the age of grace, the church age, although they dearly wanted to see and to understand it.

> For I tell you, that many prophets and kings have desired to see those things which ye see, and have not seen them; and to hear those things which ye hear, and have not heard them. (Luke 10:24)

> Of which salvation the prophets have inquired and searched diligently, who prophesied of the *grace that should come unto you.* (1 Peter 1:10, emphasis mine)

Even the angels desired to look into this grace of salvation per 1 Peter 1:12.

As God's children, we have a birthright and are privileged to be given access to all his benefits and blessings as we pray and search God's Word and depend upon the Holy Spirit to reveal his will to us so that we may let others see Jesus in all that we do and say.

> Now we have received, not the spirit of the world, but the spirit which is of God; *that we might know the things that are freely given to us of God.* (1 Corinthians 2:12, emphasis mine)

Don't forget to put your name in the scriptures when studying God's Word where you see the words *we, us, our, you, ye, saints,* and *brethren*. This will encourage you and make God's benefits real to you.

We are given all things that we need as Christians. Please notice the phrases *all* and *all things* in the scriptures as we list a few of them in this section.

> He that spared not his own Son, but delivered him up *for us all*, how shall he not with him also *freely give us all things*? (Romans 8:32, emphasis mine)

> Grace and peace be multiplied unto you through the knowledge of God, and of Jesus our Lord, according as his divine power hath given to us *all things that pertain unto life and godliness, through the knowledge of him that hath called us to glory and virtue*: Whereby are given to us exceeding great and precious promises: that by these ye might be partakers of the divine nature having escaped the corruption that is in the world through lust. And beside this, giving all diligence, add to your faith virtue; and to virtue knowledge; and to knowledge patience; and to patience godliness; and to godliness brotherly kindness; and to brotherly kindness charity. For if these things be in you, and abound, they make you that ye shall neither be barren nor unfruitful in the knowledge of our Lord Jesus Christ. *But he that lacketh these things is blind, and cannot see afar off, and hath forgotten that he was purged from his old sins.* Wherefore the rather, brethren, *give diligence to make your calling and election sure: for if ye do these things, ye shall never fall.* (2 Peter 2–10, emphasis mine)

The very moment that we are saved, we are given the Holy Spirit and are sealed by him, signifying a finished transaction, security, and that God owns us. We are in his family.

> In whom [Jesus] ye also trusted, after that ye heard the word of truth, the gospel of your salvation: in whom also *after that ye believed, ye were sealed with the Holy Spirit of promise. Which is the earnest of our inheritance* until the redemption of the purchased possession, unto the promise of his glory. (Ephesians 1:13–14, emphasis mine)

The Holy Spirit is our down payment to assure us of our total inheritance (our glorified body and being just like Jesus) that is already paid for by Jesus's finished work on the cross.

> Howbeit when he, the Spirit of truth is come, he will guide you into *all truth*: for he shall not speak of himself; but whatsoever he shall hear, that shall he speak; and he will shew you things to come [including church doctrine]. (John 16:13, emphasis mine)

> But the comforter, which is the Holy Ghost, whom the Father will send in my name, he shall teach you *all things*, and bring *all things* to your remembrance, whatsoever I have said unto you. (John 14:26, emphasis mine)

When the Apostle Paul was talking about things that God had prepared for them who love him in the book of 1 Corinthians, he tells us that the unsaved person cannot discern the benefits that God has for us, and that shows that the believer might know our prepared blessings and benefits that are freely given to us by God through the work of the Holy Spirit, which is given to all saints at the new birth experience.

But as it is written, Eye hath not seen, nor ear
heard, neither have entered into the heart of
man [the unsaved], the things which God hath
prepared for them that love him. *But God hath
revealed them unto us [the believer] by his Spirit;*
for the Spirit searcheth *all things*, yea, the deep
things of God. *Now we have received, not the spirit
of the world, but the Spirit which is of God: that we
might know the things that are freely given to us of
God. But the natural man receiveth not the things
of the Spirit of God;* for they are foolishness unto
him: neither can he know them, because they
are spiritually discerned. *But he that is spiritual
judgeth all things*, yet he himself is judged of no
man [the unbeliever]. For who [the unbeliever]
hath known the mind of the Lord, that he may
instruct him? *But we [believers] have the mind of
Christ.* (1 Corinthians 2:9–16, emphasis mine)

Blessed be the God and Father of our Lord
Jesus Christ, *who hath* [already] *blessed us with
all spiritual blessings in heavenly places in Christ*
[we get what Christ gets—more on that later].
(Ephesians 1:3, emphasis mine)

And we know that *all things* work together for
good to them that *love God*, to them who are the
called according to his purpose. (Romans 8:28,
emphasis mine)

We take a little detour now to see what Jesus says in John's
gospel concerning those who *love God* as stated in the above verse
because it is very important for us to know as we study God's Word.

He that hath my commandments, and *keepeth
them, he it is that loveth me: and he that loveth me*

41

shall be loved of my Father, and I will love him, and will manifest myself to him. (John 14:21, emphasis mine)

Jesus answered and said unto him, *if a man love me, he will keep my words*: and my Father will love him, *and we will come unto him and make our abode with him.* (John 14:23, emphasis mine)

We may not like or understand some of the things that are happening to us or around us, but we need to remember that God's thoughts and his ways are higher than our thoughts and our ways because he knows all, sees all, and he rules, overrules, and universally rules because he is the sovereign God.

All things are working toward the return of Jesus and his kingdom, and *we know that God does everything after the counsel of his own will.*

In whom [Jesus] also we have obtained an inheritance, being predestinated according to the purpose of him [God] *who worketh all things after the counsel of his own will.* (Ephesians 1:11, emphasis mine)

We also know that God's wonderful grace is and will be sufficient for us as we, in all circumstances, abide in Christ, walk in the Spirit, and stay in fellowship with the Father, therefore, having a clear conscience toward God.

THE OLD ACCUSER

These next three verses are to bring us joy, peace, and assurance but also to make us wonder why some Christians are feeling defeated, weak, without peace, and out of fellowship with God.

> He that spared not his own Son, but delivered him up for us all, how shall he not with him *freely give us all things*? Who shall lay anything to the charge of God's elect? It is God that justifieth. Who is he that condemneth? It is Christ that died, yea rather, that is risen again, who also maketh intercession for us. (Romans 8:32–34, emphasis mine)

If God the Father justified us (declared us not guilty of sins and gave us Christ's righteousness, making us perfect in Christ, and Jesus paid for all the sins of the world and is making intercession for us at the right hand of God, being our lawyer, pleading our case) who is he then that makes us feel so guilty for our old sins, robs us of our joy, our peace, keeps us weak, condemns us, and accuses us before God?

We get the answers to all of these and other questions from the Word of God, comparing scripture with scripture.

> And the great dragon was cast out, that old serpent, called the Devil and Satan, which deceiveth the whole world: He was cast out into the earth, and his angels were cast out with him. And I heard a loud voice saying in heaven. Now is come salvation, and strength, and the kingdom of our

> God, and the power of his Christ; for the accuser
> of our brethren is cast down, which accused
> them before our God day and night. (Revelation
> 12:9–10)

You see, our penalty and the guilt for our sins were paid for and forgotten by the work on the cross, which Jesus did for our salvation, and we can be certain that it is true because on the cross, Jesus said, "It is finished." There's absolutely nothing left to be done for salvation. Ever!

Satan is the one accusing us to the Father and also tempting us to revert back to the old Adam nature, which satisfies the lust of the eye, the lust of the flesh, and the pride of life, tempting us to do evil, which is anything that displeases God and exalts man.

Satan's goal is to keep us defeated (dwelling on past sins and to hide God's truth from us concerning our birthright benefits that God freely gives to all believers), thereby killing our witness and the victory that we have in our great salvation and stealing our assurance and boldness that is ours in Christ.

How can we keep from being defeated by Satan and his demons? Our defense for the battle and the temptations from Satan is the same one used by Jesus when he was tempted in the wilderness. We can see how he overcame in this scripture:

> And Jesus being full of the Holy Ghost returned
> from Jordan, and was led by the Spirit into the
> wilderness, being forty days tempted of the devil.
> And in those days he did eat nothing; and when
> they were ended, he afterward hungered. And the
> devil said unto him, If thou be the Son of God,
> command this stone that it be made bread. And
> Jesus answered him, saying *It is written*, that man
> shall not live by bread alone, but by every word of
> God. And the devil, taking him up into an high
> mountain, shewed unto him all the kingdoms of
> the world in a moment of time. And the devil

said unto him, All this power will I give thee, and
the glory of them: For that is delivered unto me;
and to whomsoever I will give it. If thou therefore wilt worship me, all shall be thine. And Jesus
answered and said unto him, Get thee behind
me, Satan: For *it is written*, thou shalt worship
the Lord thy God, and him only shalt thou serve.
And he brought him to Jerusalem, and set him
on a pinnacle of the temple, and said unto him,
if thou be the Son of God, cast thyself down from
hence: For it is written, he shall give his angels
charge over thee, to keep thee: And in their hands
they shall bear thee up, lest at any time thou dash
thy foot against a stone. And Jesus answering
said unto him, *It is said*, thou shalt not tempt the
Lord thy God. And when the devil had ended
all the temptation, he departed from him for a
season. (Luke 4:1–13, emphasis mine)

For each temptation Jesus said, "it is written" or "it is said"
and quoted the appropriate scripture in rebuttal of each temptation,
thereby defeating Satan in each encounter. Therefore, our defense is
the Word of God and the whole armor of God, that we find in the
following scripture:

Finally, my brethren, be strong in the Lord and
the power of his might. Put on the whole armor
of God, that ye may be able to stand against the
wiles of the devil. For we wrestle not against flesh
and blood, but against principalities, against
powers, against the rulers of the darkness of
this world, against spiritual wickedness in high
places. Wherefore take unto you the whole armor
of God, that ye may be able to withstand in the
evil day, and having done all to stand. Stand
therefore, having your loins girt about with *truth*,

and having on the *breastplate of righteousness*; and your feet shod with the preparation of the *gospel of peace*; Above all, taking the *shield of faith*, wherewith ye shall be able to quench all the fiery darts of the wicked. And take the *helmet of salvation*, and *the sword of the Spirit, which is the word of God: Praying always* with all prayer and supplication *in the Spirit, and watching thereunto* with all perseverance and supplication for all saints; (Ephesians 6:10–18, emphasis mine)

Now that we know *who* we are battling (Satan), *what* we are battling (temptation and fiery darts), *when* we are battling (constantly, he accuses us day and night), *why* we are battling (to keep our joy, peace, our testimony, our prayers heard, to keep our continual fellowship with God, and to have a clear conscience), the most important question we need to ask is *where* do these battles take place?

Is the battle in the home with the wife or husband or children? No.

Is the battle in the workplace with the boss or with fellow workers? No.

Is the battle with governments, local or national? No.

Is the battle with church authority or with fellow Christians? No.

If not in any of these places, *where* is the battle fought? We find that answer in 2 Corinthians.

For though we walk in the flesh we do not war after the flesh: [using human means] (For the weapons of our warfare are not carnal, [guns, clubs, knives, or bombs etc.] but mighty through God to the pulling down of strongholds) Casting down *imaginations*, and every high thing that exalteth itself against the *knowledge* of God, and bringing into captivity every *thought* to the obedience of Christ. (2 Corinthians 10:3–5, emphasis mine)

Think about it. Where do *imaginations, knowledge, and thoughts* take place, but in our thinking processes, the mind, and from the mind to the heart, then to the will and to the emotions. So the battles we fight are within ourselves and not from the outside.

Our weapons (God's Word and prayer) are all we need for the victory when we do battle against Satan and his army of demons. But we must know God's Word and how to rightly divide it to repel Satan's temptations and his darts. We have to prepare ahead of time so that we will be ready for him.

> For the word of God is quick [alive] and powerful, and sharper than any two edged sword, piercing even to the dividing asunder of soul and spirit and is a discerner of thoughts and intents of the heart. (Hebrews 4:12)

This verse should give you comfort and assurance that through diligent study of God's Word and retaining it in your heart and mind, you will be well equipped for your battles when you are tempted by Satan. After all, that is the way in which Jesus overcame his temptations, and Jesus is our example in all things. He is the yardstick we all have to measure ourselves by.

The who, when, what, why, and where are important questions, but what's most important is how to use our defensive armor and how to use God's Word in our battles to overcome Satan's wiles and for God's glory, and not for our own glory.

ACCESS TO GOD
THE FATHER

All the sons and daughters in God's family are truly blessed with birthright benefits in that they may approach God by prayer at any time through Jesus Christ, our high priest, who sits at the right hand of the Father, making intercession for us.

Keep in mind that under the law, only the high priest could enter into the holy of holies, where the glory of God rests above the mercy seat and that just once a year, on the day of atonement, to make an offering for the sins of the people with a blood sacrifice. But first, he had to offer a blood sacrifice for himself and wash his hands and his feet before performing his priestly duties for the people, passing by the lampstand (signifying Jesus as the light of the world) and passing by the table of showbread (signifying Jesus as the bread of life), then on to the altar of incense where a sweet-smelling mixture of spices were being burned (representing the prayers of the people), and then on into the holy of holies, sprinkling blood roundabout to purify everything. Then would God speak with the high priest from above the mercy seat, revealing his will for his people, Israel.

> And thou shalt put the mercy seat above upon the ark; and in the ark thou shalt put the testimony that I shall give thee. And there I will meet with thee, and I will commune with thee from above the mercy seat, from between the two cherubims which are upon the ark of the testimony, of all things which I will give thee in command-

ment unto the children of Israel [his will for the
people]. (Exodus 25:21–22)

The duties of the priests were very serious business to God and
had to be carried out in a specially prescribed manner to please him.

God gave Moses exact and very detailed instructions on how to
construct the tabernacle, and the materials to be used for each item,
and even the color of each material; but he didn't stop there. He also
prescribed in detail how every priest should be clothed and how they
should offer up all sacrifices, no exceptions!

We have an example of just how serious God was concerning
the priest's approach to himself. As we can see in these scriptures.

> And Nadab and Abihu, the sons of Aaron, took
> either of them his censer, and put fire therein,
> and put incense thereon, and offered strange fire
> before the Lord, which he commanded them
> not. And there went out fire from the Lord, and
> devoured them, and they died before the Lord.
> (Leviticus 10:1–2)

> And the Lord spoke unto Moses, saying, Thou
> shalt also make a laver of brass, and his foot also
> of brass, to wash withal: and thou shalt put it
> between the tabernacle of the congregation and
> the altar, and thou shalt put water therein. For
> Aaron and his sons shall wash their hands and
> their feet thereat: When they go into the taber-
> nacle of the congregation, they shall wash with
> water, *that they die not*; or when they come near
> to the altar to minister, to burn offering made by
> fire unto the Lord: *So they shall wash their hands
> and their feet, that they die not*; and it shall be
> a statute for ever to them, even to him and to
> his seed throughout their generations. (Exodus
> 30:17–21, emphasis mine)

Was God serious about the priest's approach to himself for fellowship and for finding out his will for them? Absolutely, for sure, he was then, and he is still serious today. Priests (saints) have to be perfect and righteous to enter into the presence of the holy and righteous God. Sounds impossible, doesn't it? But don't fret; God has already provided his remedy for us and our sins, and the qualifications for our fellowship, and our service, and for our worship.

> If we say that we have no sin, we deceive ourselves, and the truth is not in us. *If we confess our sins, he is faithful and just to forgive us our sins, and to cleanse us from all unrighteousness.* If we say that we have not sinned, we make him a liar, and his word is not in us. (1 John 1:8–10, emphasis mine)

When God cleanses us from all unrighteousness (as his word says), then we are righteous and perfect and ready for fellowship with God, ready to study his Word, ready to worship, and ready to have our prayers heard and answered.

We are the tabernacle of God in this age of grace, and we are the priests that minister in our tabernacles (all this worship, fellowship, studying, sacrifice, and our prayers are generated from within us by the Holy Spirit).

First, the sacrifices that we offer are found in these scriptures.

> I beseech you therefore, brethren, by the mercies of God, that ye present your bodies a living sacrifice, holy, acceptable unto God, which is your reasonable service. And be not conformed to this world: *but be ye transformed by the renewing of your mind*, that ye may prove what is that good, and acceptable, and perfect, will of God. (Romans 12:1–2, emphasis mine)

By him [Jesus] therefore let us offer the sacrifice
of praise to God continually, that is, the fruit of
our lips giving thanks to his name. But to do
good and to communicate [share with others]
forget not: for with such sacrifices God is well
pleased. (Hebrews 13:15–16)

For all the law is fulfilled in one word, even in
this; Thou shalt love thy neighbor as thyself.
(Galatians 5:14)

As we act out of love to others, there are many more sacrifices
that we will make when we minister our gifts for others' benefit and
for God's glory.

Second, we wash, confessing our sins (as already stated in 1 John
1:8–9) for cleansing; also, we see our need in the following scriptures:

If I regard iniquity in my heart, the Lord will not
hear me. (Psalm 66:18)

For all have sinned and come short of the glory of
God. (Romans 3:23)

If all of us have missed the mark of not measuring up to the
standard of the glory of God, *what is God's standard that we must
meet to please him?* God's word makes that very plain in the following
scriptures:

God, who at sundry times and in divers manners spake in times past unto the fathers by the
prophets, hath in these last days spoken unto us
by his Son, whom he hath appointed heir of all
things, by whom also he made the worlds; *who
being the brightness of his glory, and the express
image of his person,* and upholding all things by
the word of his power, when he had by himself

purged [removed] our sins, sat down on the right hand of the majesty on high. (Hebrews 1:1–3, emphasis mine)

For God, who commanded the light to shine out of darkness, hath shined in our hearts, to give *the light of the knowledge of the glory of God in the face of Jesus Christ.* (2 Corinthians 4:6, emphasis mine)

So then if we haven't measured up to the glory of God (Jesus) in our motives, our deeds, our speech, our attitude, and our love for others in all situations and opportunities, we must wash (confess our sins to be righteous) before we can enter into the holy place to allow Jesus to enlighten us (the lampstand) and to feed on the showbread (Jesus, the Word of God), then according to the knowledge that pleases God, we may go on further to the altar of incense and offer up prayers that are acceptable to him.

All true believers are priests in this age of grace as told in this scripture.

But ye are a chosen generation, a royal priesthood, an holy nation, a peculiar people; that ye should shew forth the praises of him who hath called you out of darkness, into his marvelous light: Which in time past were not a people, but are now the people of God, which had not obtained mercy, but now have obtained mercy. (1 Peter 2:9–10)

The sacrifice has been made, and we have washed our hands and our feet (confessed our sins and been made righteous) and have entered into the holy place and have offered up our prayer to God the Father through Jesus the Son (our high priest). How do we know for sure and without a doubt that God has heard our prayer and will absolutely positively answer it? The answer to that question and super good news for us is found in the following scriptures:

> Ask, and it shall be given you; seek and you will find; knock and it shall be opened unto you; for every one that asketh receiveth; and he that seeketh findeth; and to him that knocketh it shall be opened [talking about that which is holy; God's word; in verse 6]. (Matthew 7:7–8)

> And all things, whatsoever ye shall ask in prayer, believing, ye shall receive. (Matthew 21:22)

> And whatsoever ye shall ask in my name, that will I do, that the Father may be glorified in the Son, If ye shall ask any thing in my name, I will do it [a prayer in Jesus's name is a prayer that Jesus would pray]. (John 14:13–14)

> And this is the confidence that we have in him, that if we ask any thing according to his will, he heareth us: and if we know that he hear us, whatsoever we ask, we know that we have the petitions that we desired of him. (1 John 5:14–15)

The gist of these scriptures tells us that any child of God who is cleansed (humble, sins confessed, and made righteous) and praying in Jesus's name and praying according to the will of God will receive their request. And here is why: Jesus gave us the answer in his prayers in the garden of Gethsemane. Three times he prayed to this end.

> And he went a little farther, and fell on his face, and prayed, saying, o my Father, if it be possible, let this cup pass from me: nevertheless not as I will, but as thou wilt. (Matthew 26:39)

He prayed for God's will to be done, not his own will to be done. And he was serious as we should be also.

God is sovereign, doing anything he wants to do any time he wants, to anyone he wants, any manner he wants, anywhere he wants; and nothing or nobody can stop him from doing his will, and *God does not ask or take advice from anyone!*

> In whom [Jesus] also we have obtained an inheritance, being predestinated according to the purpose of him *[God] who worketh all things after the counsel of his own will.* (Ephesians 1:11, emphasis mine)

Therefore, when we pray a prayer that Jesus would pray (in Jesus's name) and seriously and truly in our hearts submit our will unto God's will (as Jesus always did), then our prayer is instantly answered. And we know it is answered, and then we can claim the victory because God always does his will.

> Likewise the Spirit also helpeth our infirmities: For we know not what we should pray for as we ought: but the Spirit itself [himself] maketh intercession for us with groanings which cannot be uttered. And he that searcheth the hearts knoweth what is the mind of the Spirit, because he maketh intercession for the saints according to the will of God. (Romans 8:26–27)

Another added assurance for us is that God never strains or struggles to do anything. He either does what he wants, or it was never in his will, plus he is always right; he knows all and never has he made a mistake.

> Then came the word of the Lord unto Jeremiah, saying, Behold, I am the Lord, the God of

all flesh: is there any thing too hard for me?
(Jeremiah 32:26–27)

Ask yourself this: Does God the Father say no to Jesus's prayers?
No! Never once has God rejected a prayer that Jesus prayed. Does
God say maybe to Jesus's prayers? Absolutely not! Does God say for
Jesus to wait a while for the answer to his prayer? No, because as soon
as a true prayer is offered up (one that is truly in Jesus's name and one
that truly wants God's will to be done), we can be sure it is answered
because God always does his will no matter if anyone opposes it or
not; nobody can contend with God and win! (God's word does not
lie to us.)

After being asked, Jesus taught his disciples how to pray.

> And when thou prayest, thou shalt not be as the
> hypocrites are; for they love to pray standing in the
> synagogues and in the corners of the streets that
> they may be seen of men. Verily I say unto you,
> they have their reward. But when thou prayest,
> enter into thy closet, and when thou hast shut
> thy door, pray to the Father which is in secret;
> and thy Father which seeth in secret shall reward
> thee openly. But when ye pray, use not vain rep-
> etitions, as the heathen do: For they think that
> they shall be heard for their much speaking. Be
> ye not therefore like unto them: For your Father
> knoweth what things ye have need of, before ye
> ask him [we cannot inform God of anything that
> he doesn't already know!]. (Matthew 6:5–8)

Jesus said not to use vain (worthless) repetitions, which is praying the same prayers over and over, day in and day out, year in and
year out. Praying like that just confirms that we don't trust God's
will to be what is best and what is right for his purposes and for the
believer's good, that we think that we know what is better for us than

he does (that is the pride of life thinking, the old Adam sinful nature that is in us.)

> Ye lust, and have not: ye kill, and desire to have, and cannot obtain: ye fight and war, yet ye have not, because ye ask not. Ye ask, and receive not, because ye ask amiss, that ye may consume it upon your lusts [wanting our own selfish will done, and not for God's will to be done]. (James 4:2–3)

We need to always ask ourselves, Am I smarter than God? Am I more informed than God? The answer is always no! So why not rely on God's will to be done in all instances? He has never made a mistake yet, and he never will.

When Jesus was in the garden of Gethsemane, he prayed the will of the Father to be done all three times. And Jesus is our example in all things and calls for his disciples to "*follow me*" (do like I do).

Does this teaching go against the traditional teaching in our churches today?

Sure, it does. But are we going to embrace the old traditions of man and denominations, or are we going to trust what God's Word says?

> And we know that all things work together for good to them that love God. To them who are the called according to his purpose. (Romans 8:28)

> Trust in the Lord with all thine heart; and lean not to thine own understanding. In all thy ways acknowledge him, and he shall direct thy paths. Be not wise in thine own eyes: fear the Lord, and depart from evil. (Proverbs 3:5–7)

> Wherefore be ye not unwise, but understanding what the will of the Lord is. (Ephesians 5:17)

Our privilege and duty is to use our knowledge and our freely given gifts to please and bring honor to God, not to please ourselves or mankind. Remember, we rise or fall in fellowship, joy, peace, and a clear conscience according to our believing God's word enough to allow the Holy Spirit to put it to work in our daily life.

Believe God's word—receive his blessings.

Reject God's word—receive his condemnation.

But what about public prayer, and what is its purpose? Jesus's teaching was for us to pray in secret (Matthew chapter 6:6). Jesus did pray in public but not very often. We need to look at some of his prayers to find out why he prayed openly. At Lazarus's tomb, Jesus lifted up his eyes and said, "Father, I thank thee that thou hast heard me."

> And I knew that thou hearest me always: but *because of the people which stand by I said it*, that they may believe that thou hast sent me. (John 11:42, emphasis mine)

> And it came to pass, that, as he was praying in a certain place, when he ceased, one of his disciples said unto him, Lord, teach us to pray, as John also taught his disciples. (Luke 11:1)

The prayer that followed was a teaching prayer, said for the benefit of his disciples. If they had been hearing him pray in public, they would have already known how to pray. Would they not?

The high priestly prayer in John chapter 17 was also a teaching prayer by Jesus, telling the disciples what to expect later, which was that he was sending them out into the world as the Father had sent him (verse 20 included all believers), and that he and the Father would be in them and they all would be one, and that they might have Jesus's joy fulfilled in themselves (verse 13), and that God the Father would keep them from the evil (verse 15).

> Likewise the Spirit also helpeth our infirmities [weaknesses]: for we know not what we should

pray for as we ought: but the Spirit itself [himself] maketh intercession for us with groanings which cannot be uttered. And he that searcheth the hearts knoweth what is the mind of the Spirit, because he maketh intercession for the saints according to the will of God. (Romans 8:26–27)

You can see from the above verses that the Holy Spirit and God the Father are in perfect communication with each other, not according to our feeble words because we don't know what we should pray for as we ought (we don't know all things yet), and our words are not perfect, but the Holy Spirit takes a reading on what is in our hearts and then relays that to God the Father in accordance with his will, and that with groanings that we don't hear.

Jesus's public prayers were revealing himself as the Messiah and showing the people that he was humbling himself and was relying on God the Father for his words and for the power to perform all his miracles, signs, and the wonders that he did (they were teaching prayers).

His prayers were for them and for us to rely on God for all our needs and strength for our Christian living.

Giving thanks always for all things unto God and the Father in the name of our Lord Jesus Christ. (Ephesians 5:20, emphasis mine)

In every thing give thanks: for this is the will of God in Christ concerning you. (1 Thessalonians 5:18)

Therefore, our public prayers are for the benefit of those listening, teaching them how to pray, to keep a humble and thankful heart, confessing their sins, and giving glory to God for his abiding presence that is in them forever, praying earnestly for God's will to be done in all things, always in Jesus's name. Public prayers are beneficial for all who hear but chiefly for believers who haven't matured in the Word as yet, but also for a witness to the unbelievers, convicting them of their sins and that they need salvation to partake in all God's blessings.

Access to God through prayers in Jesus's name is one of our most glorious benefits. All believers have the same wonderful access, and he desires their fellowship with himself.

> Behold, I stand at the door, and knock: If any man hear my voice, and open the door, I will come in to him, and will sup with him, and he with me. (Revelation 3:20)

We only have to ask, seek, and knock. God is always ready for our fellowship.

HEIRS AND JOINT HEIRS WITH JESUS CHRIST

First of all, an heir in God's family is one of his children who is in line to inherit something at some point, but it is not merited; it is wholly a gift from God. All believers qualify for these inheritances due to their born-again experience through Jesus's finished work on the cross.

> And because ye are sons, God hath sent forth the Spirit of his Son into your hearts, crying, Abba Father. Wherefore thou art no more a servant, but a son; and if a son, then an heir of God through Christ. (Galatians 4:6–7)

In Ephesians 1:3–4, God's word tells us that *we already have the down payment of our full inheritance, which is the indwelling Holy Spirit.*

First Peter 1:3–4 tells us that we have an incorruptible, undefiled inheritance that doesn't fade away, reserved for us, the believers.

> The spirit itself [himself] beareth witness with our spirit, that we are the children of God, and if children, then heirs; heirs of God, and joint heirs with Christ; if so be that we suffer with him, that we may be also glorified together. (Romans 8:16–17)

> For whom he did foreknow [the believer], he also
> did predestinate to be conformed to the image
> of his Son, that he might be the firstborn among
> many brethren. (Romans 8:29)

God has said that we are going to be just like Jesus, and we are
in the process of that very thing as we humble ourselves, study God's
Word, believe God's Word enough to allow the Holy Spirit and his
power to lead us so that others will see Jesus in all that we do and say.
Follow him.

What Jesus gets, we get. We shall share in all his glory because
we are in him and he is in us. We are his bride; we have become one
in him.

Here are a few scriptures that tell us parts of our inheritance;
hopefully, they will encourage you and excite you.

> Do ye not know that the saints shall judge the
> world? Know ye not that we shall judge angels?
> How much more things that pertain to this life?
> (1 Corinthians 6:2–3)

> To him that overcometh, will I grant to sit with
> me in my throne, even as I overcame, and am set
> down with my Father in his throne. He that hath
> an ear let him hear what the Spirit saith unto the
> churches. (Revelation 3:21–22)

In Luke 19, Jesus gave us the parable of the ten pounds and
the servants. The servant that took one pound and gained ten more
pounds was commended by Jesus.

> And he said unto him, well, thou good servant:
> *because thou hast been faithful in a very little,*
> have thou authority over ten cities. (Luke 19:17,
> emphasis mine)

In Matthew 25, the servant was entrusted with five talents, and he gained five other talents, and we can see how he was rewarded.

> His lord said unto him, well done, thou good and faithful servant: thou hast been faithful over *a few things*, I will make thee ruler *many things*; enter thou into the joy of thy lord. (Matthew 25:21, emphasis mine)

Only overcomers and the ones who have ears to hear will understand and partake of these wonderful inheritances. They are guaranteed to us in God's word, but if we don't feed on God's word and find out what God has freely given to us as heirs of God and joint heirs with Christ, we cannot fully experience the assurance, and joy, and peace, and soul rest that come from knowing and claiming our blessed inheritance.

> He that spared not his own Son, but delivered him up *for us all, how shall he not with him also freely give us all things?* (Romans 8:32, emphasis mine)

We have listed only a few inheritances; look for many more as you study God's Word. You will be thrilled by each new benefit you find, and be sure to share them with others. God will bless you if you do.

THE FIRSTBORN IN
GOD'S FAMILY

We can see from the scripture (Romans 8:29) that we are predestined to be just like Jesus, *the firstborn among many brethren* and that we will share in all things with him as heir and a joint heir. But before we get the big head and develop an extra-large ego and think that we are holier and above all others and can tell Jesus what to do, we need to consider what the scriptures say concerning the doctrine of the firstborn.

What is the advantage of the firstborn? We go to the Old Testament for the answer to this question.

> If a man have two wives, one beloved, and another hated, and they have born him children, both the beloved and the hated: and if the firstborn son be hers that was hated: then it shall be, when he maketh his sons to inherit that which he hath, that he may not make the son of the beloved firstborn before the son of the hated, which is indeed the firstborn: but he shall acknowledge the son of the hated for the firstborn; *by giving him a double portion of all that he hath*: for he is the beginning of his strength; the right of the firstborn is his. (Deuteronomy 21:15–17, emphasis mine)

Before the Aaronic priesthood was established, the spiritual head of the family was the father. At the death of the father or the dividing of his estate, the spiritual headship as well as the double portion of the inheritance fell to the firstborn son (this was known as the birthright). We have a birthright by being born into the family of God and all believers are priests, *but we are not the high priest*; that would be Jesus, the firstborn from the dead, the only begotten Son in John 3:16.

We see an example of the birthright and the double portion when we look at Esau and Jacob. Esau was indeed the firstborn but did not regard the birthright (the spiritual headship of the family) as of any value and traded it to Jacob for a bowl of soup. On the other hand, Jacob had faith that it was of great importance and gladly took it (Esau had no faith; Jacob showed faith).

The double portion was an entirely different matter for Esau. He dearly wanted it because Isaac was a very rich man, and he would receive a large inheritance (twice as much as Jacob's). But Jacob, through trickery and deception, stole the blessing from Esau, making him mad enough to kill, but it was too late; the double portion had already been bestowed on Jacob.

Jesus is the firstborn Son of God, and he is the spiritual head of all believers, and he is indeed our high priest, and we are under his authority. Only through Jesus and his shed blood and in his name can we pray to the Father and gain access into his presence.

We are married to him, and as the groom, he is the head of his bride, the church.

> And he [Jesus] is the head of the body, the church; who is the beginning, the firstborn from the dead; that in all things he might have the pre-eminence [first place]. For it pleased the Father that in him should all fullness dwell. (Colossians 1:18–19)

Since Jesus is indeed the firstborn and has all authority over all Christians, we are told how to live our lives in order to please God the Father.

> And whatsoever ye do in word or deed, do all in the name of the Lord Jesus, giving thanks to God and the Father by him [Lord means supreme authority]. (Colossians 3:17)

All things we say and do, if they please God, we have to do them in the same spirit, attitude, and in the same motivation that Jesus had. Always be humble, in love and obedience.

Double portion example: If a man had ten sons, he would divide the inheritance into eleven shares; therefore, nine sons would receive one share each, and *the firstborn would receive two shares,* for a total of eleven shares. *Thus, the firstborn son was receiving a double portion.*

MATURING IN CHRIST—
OUR NEW THINGS

> Therefore if any man be in Christ, he is a new
> creature: old things are passed away; behold, all
> things become new. (2 Corinthians 5:17)

When we are born from above (spiritually), we are babes in Christ;
just as in a natural birth, we are born babies, and like natural babies,
we feed on milk for a while and then on soft food, and finally, we
need solid food, such as meat and vegetables, to grow strong and
healthy. All of these stages that we go through are necessary for us to
mature and become all that we should be and all that we could be
physically and also spiritually.

The scriptures tell us how to feed as babes in Christ and also
how we are to progress through all the stages of growth until we reach
maturity.

> Wherefore laying aside all malice, and guile, and
> hypocrites, and envies, and all evil speaking, as
> newborn babes, desire the sincere milk of the
> word, that ye may grow thereby. (1 Peter 2:1–2)

As in verse one, we have to sacrifice and humble ourselves
before we will receive the promise of growth as stated in verse two;
that is the first step toward maturity. But God didn't stop there; he
gave gifts unto men and also gave the gifted men to the church for
the purpose of teaching and leading his children on their journey to
maturity. That journey's goal is to become more and more like our

Lord Jesus Christ as we feed on God's word and grow. We see that process outlined in Ephesians.

> But to every one of us is given grace according to the measure of the gift of Christ. And he gave some, [churches] apostles; and some prophets; and some evangelists; and some pastors and teachers; for the perfecting [maturing] of the saints, for the work of the ministry, for the edifying of the body of Christ: till we all come in the unity of the faith, and of the knowledge of the Son of God, *unto a perfect man unto the measure of the stature of the fullness of Christ*: that we henceforth be no more children, tossed to and fro, and carried about with every wind of doctrine, by the sleight of men, and cunning craftiness, whereby they lie in wait to deceive. *But speaking the truth in love, may grow up into him in all things, which is the head, even Christ.* (Ephesians 4:7,11–15)

Jesus said when talking to the scribes and pharisees in John:

> Search the scriptures; for in them ye think ye have eternal life: and they are they that testify of me. (John 5:39)

If we ever attain unto spiritual maturity, we will only do it through feeding on God's word, by humbling ourselves, and diligently studying as the Apostle Paul instructed Timothy in these passages:

> Study to show thyself approved unto God, a workman that needeth not to be ashamed, rightly dividing the word of truth. (2 Timothy 2:15)

> All scripture is given by inspiration of God, and
> is profitable for doctrine [teaching], for reproof,
> for correction, for instruction in righteousness;
> that the man of God may be perfect, thoroughly
> furnished unto all good works. (2 Timothy
> 3:16–17)

When we are born again and baptized into the body of Christ and have received the Holy Spirit to dwell in us forever, truly, all things are new to us like a newborn baby. It is a whole new world out there, and we need to find out what it is all about and how we fit into it and what our benefits as the children of God are.

> Bless the Lord o my soul and forget not all his
> benefits. (Psalm 103:2)

> He that spared not his own Son, but delivered
> him up for us all, how shall he not with him also
> freely give us all things? (Romans 8:32)

Now, as Christians, we need to explore this new world and all of God's benefits that he has provided for all his children. They are new to us, and all of them are ours by birthright. To know and claim (through faith) our new benefits will assure us of God's continuing love for us, for our peace, our joy, our security, and for our growth toward maturity.

Next, we have listed a few of those new things that are ours to enjoy and can and will be real to us when we receive them through faith.

- We have a new Father.

> And what agreement hath the temple of God
> with idols? For *ye are the temple of the living God*:
> As God hath said, *I will dwell in them, and walk
> in them; and I will be their God, and they shall*

be my people. Wherefore come out from among them, and be ye separate, saith the Lord and touch not the unclean thing: and I will receive you, and *will be a Father unto you, and ye shall be my sons and daughters, saith the Lord almighty.* (2 Corinthians 6:16–18, emphasis mine)

How are we going to top that promise?

- We have a new family.

  Behold, what manner of love the Father hath bestowed upon us, that we should be called the sons of God: therefore the world knoweth us not, because it knew him not. Beloved, now are we the sons of God, and it doth not yet appear what we shall be; but we know that, when he shall appear, *we shall be like him: for we shall see him as he is.* (1 John 3:1–2, emphasis mine)

  The Spirit itself [himself] beareth witness with our spirit, that we are the children of God: and if children, then heirs; heirs of God, and joint heirs with Christ [*we get what Jesus gets!*]. (Romans 8:16–17)

- We have a new nature.

  Grace and peace be multiplied unto you *through the knowledge of God, and of Jesus our Lord.* According as his divine power (the Holy Spirit) hath [already] *given to us* all things that pertain into life and godliness, through the knowledge of him that hath called us to glory and virtue: whereby are given to us exceeding great and precious promises; that by these ye might be partakers of *the divine nature*, having escaped the corruption that is in the world through lust. (2 Peter 1:2–4, emphasis mine)

God has made available to all believers his divine nature, and it is at war with the old Adam nature. But notice that we get the divine nature from the *knowledge of God and Jesus* that is revealed to us *by the Holy Spirit and his power,* not by any power of our own and not by man (the unbeliever). It is up to each believer to humble himself or herself and ask, seek, and knock through prayer, meditation, and study, and obedience to God's word to receive this wonderful knowledge that brings to him or her a new divine nature.

- We have new promises.

There are many promises that are given to us in the scriptures, but they have to be believed and claimed before they can be received. We are listing only a few verses of his promises here, but you can find many more as you study God's Word.

For whatsoever is born of God overcometh the world: and this is the victory that overcometh the world, even our faith. (1 John 5:4)

To him that overcometh, will I grant to sit with me in my throne, even as I also overcame, and am set down with my Father in his throne. (Revelation 3:21)

Do ye not know that the saints shall judge the world? And if the world shall be judged by you, are ye unworthy to judge the smallest matters? Know ye not that we shall judge angels? How much more things that pertain to this life? (1 Corinthians 6:2–3)

If ye abide in me, and my words abide in you, ye shall ask what you will, and It shall be done unto you. (John 15:7)

And we know that all things work together for good to them that love God, to them who are the called according to his purpose. *For whom he did foreknow, he also did predestinate to be conformed to the image of his Son,* that he might be the first-born among many brethren. He that spared not his own Son, but delivered him up for us all, *how shall he not with him also freely give us all things?* (Romans 8:28–29, 32, emphasis mine)

It's already settled; all true believers are going to be just like Jesus. And all things are ours by believing and obeying God's word; therefore, all God's promises are real and just waiting on us to receive them.

- We have a new Spirit.

And because ye are sons, God hath sent forth the Spirit of his Son into your hearts, crying, Abba, Father. (Galatians 4:6)

So then they that are in the flesh cannot please God. But ye are not in the flesh, but in the Spirit, if so be the Spirit of God dwell in you, *Now if any man have not the Spirit Of Christ, he is none of his.* (Romans 8:8–9, emphasis mine)

Now we have received, not the spirit of the world, but the Spirit which is of God; that we might know the things that are freely given to us of God. (1 Corinthians 2:12)

> For God hath not given us the spirit of fear; but of power, and of love, and of a sound mind. (2 Timothy 1:7)

The Holy Spirit is our present down payment of our later inheritance, our glorified body, just like Jesus's body.

- We have a new mind.

  > But the natural Man [unsaved] receiveth not the things of the Spirit of God: for they are foolishness unto him: neither can he know them, because they are spiritually discerned. But he that is Spiritual judgeth all things, yet he himself is judged of no man. For who [the unbeliever] hath known the mind of the Lord, that he may instruct him? But we [the believers] have the mind of Christ. (1 Corinthians 2:14–16)

  > Let this mind be in you, which was also in Christ Jesus: who being in the form of God, thought it not robbery to be equal with God: and being found in fashion as a man, he humbled himself, and became obedient unto death, even the death of the cross. (Philippians 2:5–6, 8)

Even though believers have God the Father, God the Son, and God the Holy Spirit living in them, all believers are to humble themselves and be obedient to the will of God the Father, just as Jesus did in all things. He set the example for us to follow.

Ask yourself this question: If it wasn't possible to have the same mind that Jesus had in humbling himself in his obedience to God the Father's will, why would the Word of God challenge us to do likewise? It's a matter of choice for each of us; we can choose to please God or our own selfish desires. We are all under the same test.

- We have a new teacher.

But the comforter, which is the Holy Ghost, whom the Father will send in my name, *he shall teach you all things*, and bring to your remembrance, whatsoever I have said unto you. (John 14:26, emphasis mine)

I have yet many things to say unto you, but ye cannot bear them now. *Howbeit when he, the Holy Spirit of truth, is come, he will guide you into all truth*; for he shall not speak of himself; but whatsoever he shall hear, that shall he speak; *and he will shew you things to come.* He shall glorify me: for he shall receive of mine, and shall shew it unto you. All things that the Father hath are mine: therefore said I, that he shall take of mine, and shall shew it unto you. (John 16:12–15, emphasis mine)

But ye have an unction from the Holy one, and ye know all things. But the anointing which ye have received of him abideth in you, *and ye need not that any man [unbeliever] teach you: but as the same anointing teacheth you of all things, and is truth, and is no lie, and even as it (he) hath taught you, ye shall abide in him.* (1 John 2:20, 27, emphasis mine)

Men may stand and proclaim the Word of God, but the Holy Spirit is giving the power and the words that bring glory to God. All of our efforts are worthwhile only when they are generated by the Holy Spirit. We cannot take the credit for any words or deeds that minister our free gifts that are used through our love for God and our love for others.

For it is *God which worketh in you both the will and to do* of his good pleasure. (Philippians 2:13, emphasis mine)

- We have a new home.

Jesus was praying for his disciples in John chapter 17, and in verse 20, he included all believers.

I have given them thy word; and the world hath hated them, because they are not of the world, even as I am not of the world. I pray not that thou shouldest take them out of the world, but that thou shouldest keep them from the evil. They are not of the world, even as I am not of the world. As Thou hast sent me into the world, even so have I also sent them into the world. (John 17:14–16, 18)

Dearly beloved, I beseech you as strangers and pilgrims, abstain from fleshly lusts, which war against the soul. (1 Peter 2:11)

God's Word talks about Abraham and Sarah's faith in his promises to them.

These all died in faith, not having received the promises, but having seen them afar off, and were persuaded of them, and embraced them, and confessed that they were strangers and pilgrims on the earth. (Hebrews 11:13)

Giving thanks unto the Father, which hath made us meet [able] to be partakers of the inheritance of the saints in light: who hath delivered us from the power of darkness, and hath translated us

into the kingdom of his dear Son [the kingdom
of heaven]. (Colossians 1:12–13)

For our conversation [citizenship] is in heaven;
from whence also we look for the Savior, The
Lord Jesus Christ: who shall change our vile
body, that it may be fashioned like unto his glorious body, according to the working whereby he
is able even to subdue all things unto himself.
(Philippians 3:20–21)

Before we were saved, our old home was destined to be in the
lake of fire for all eternity with the devil and his demons, but by
believing in Jesus's death, burial, and his resurrection and his offering
of his own sinless, righteous blood to pay for our sins as well as the
sins of the whole world, that faith brings us into the family of God
and qualifies us for a new home in heaven with our loving God for
all eternity.

- We have new fruit.

Christians bear good fruit, not evil fruit, as in the days before
we were born into the family of God. Anything that we do or say or
think on, if it glorifies God the Father or God the Son, is good fruit;
anything that is not pleasing to God is evil fruit. Jesus gave us some
insight into good fruit as compared to evil fruit and also a warning
when he taught the sermon on the mount.

Beware of false prophets, which come to you in
sheep's clothing, but inwardly they are ravening
wolves Ye shall know them by their fruits. Do men
gather grapes of thorns, or figs of thistles? Even so
every good tree bringeth forth good fruit; but a
corrupt tree bringeth forth evil fruit. A good tree
cannot bring forth evil fruit, neither can a corrupt
tree bring forth good fruit. Every tree that bringeth

not forth good fruit is hewn down, and cast into the fire. Wherefore by their fruits ye shall know them. Not every one that saith unto me Lord, Lord, shall enter into the kingdom of heaven; but he that doeth the will of my Father which is in heaven. Many will say to me in that day, Lord, Lord, have we not prophesied in thy name? And in thy name have cast out devils? And in thy name done many wonderful works? And then will I profess unto them, I never knew you: depart from me, ye that work iniquity. (Matthew 7:15–23)

To bear good fruit as we journey through this life on earth, we have to be indwelt by the Holy Spirit, the very Spirit of Christ, as the Bible tells us in the following scripture:

But ye are not in the flesh, but in the Spirit, if so be that the Spirit of God dwell in you. Now if any man have not the Spirit of Christ, he is none of his. (Romans 8:9)

The fruit of the Holy Spirit versus the fruit of the natural man is clearly contrasted in the book of Galatians. The following are the things we look for in the lives of professing Christians, whether they be bishops, elders, evangelists, pastors, teachers, deacons, or any other believers.

But the fruit of the Spirit is love, joy, peace, longsuffering, gentleness, goodness, faith, meekness, temperance: against such there is no law. (Galatians 5:22)

The struggle that is within us, the old flesh nature versus the divine nature, as well as a list of evil fruits, is given in these scriptures:

For the flesh lusteth against the Spirit, and the Spirit against the flesh: and these are contrary the one to the other: so that ye cannot do the things that ye would. Now the works of the flesh are manifest, which are these; adultery, fornication, Uncleanness, lasciviousness, idolatry, witchcraft, hatred, variance, emulations, wrath, strife, seditions, heresies, envyings, murders, drunkenness, revellings and such like: of the which I tell you before, as I have also told you in time past, that they which do such things shall not inherit the kingdom of God. (Galatians 5:17,19–21)

For the kingdom of God is not meat and drink; but righteousness, and peace, and joy in the Holy Ghost. For he that in these things [bears good fruit] serveth Christ is acceptable to God, and approved of men. (Romans 14:17–18)

Beloved believe not every spirit, but try the spirits whether they are of God: because many false prophets are gone out into the world. (1 John 4:1)

Be careful, and make sure that any speaker's message and his teaching agree exactly with the scriptures and that he proclaims his message on the authority of God's Word. A true proclaimer's words and his program will always bring honor and praise to God the Father, and God the Son, and not to man and his efforts, programs, and accomplishments. We are all qualified to inspect the fruit of our leaders and teachers because we have been given the mind of Christ, the scriptures, and Christ who is our example with which to measure their fruit bearing.

Keep in mind that fruits are the love, words, deeds, attitudes, and the motives that are manifested in the lives of people. We don't have to manufacture them, put on an act, boast about them, or point them out to others; they just come out naturally. We bear them; that's our new nature. Be sensitive; look around and be aware of the good fruit that is exhibited in our family members, in our government leaders, in our church leaders, and in the lives of professing Christians. Only listen or follow the ones showing forth good fruit.

- We have new power.

  And behold, I send the promise of my Father upon you: but tarry ye in the city of Jerusalem, until ye be endued with power from on high. (Luke 24:49)

  But ye shall receive power after that the Holy Ghost is come upon you: and ye shall be witnesses unto me both in Jerusalem, and in all Judaea, and in Samaria, and unto the uttermost part of the earth. (Acts 1:8)

  For though we walk in the flesh, we do not war after the flesh:(for the weapons of our warfare are not carnal, but mighty through God to the pulling down of strong holds;) casting down *imaginations*, and every high thing that exalteth itself against the *knowledge* of God, and bringing into captivity every *thought* to the obedience of Christ. (2 Corinthians 10:3–5, emphasis mine)

  For God hath not given us the spirit of fear; but of power, and of love, and of a sound mind. (2 Timothy 1:7)

We can readily see that our power comes from the indwelling Holy Spirit given to us when we were born into the family of God. This is assured to us by the scripture that is in Galatians.

  And because ye are sons, God hath sent forth the Spirit of his Son Into your hearts, crying, Abba,

Father. Wherefore thou art no more a servant, but a son; and if a son, then an heir of God through Christ. (Galatians 4:6–7)

The Holy Spirit is our power source to be pleasing to God in our daily walk with him, letting others see Jesus in all that we say and do.

- We have a new marriage.

    Wherefore, my brethren, ye also are become dead to the law by the body of Christ; that ye should be married to another, even to him who is raised from the dead, that we should bring forth fruit unto God. (Romans 7:4)

    For I am jealous over you with godly jealousy: for I have espoused you to one husband, that I may present you as a chaste virgin to Christ. (2 Corinthians 11:2)

Our old Adam nature was a servant to the law of sin and death, but by our being in Christ on the cross, dying to the law and sin, and being resurrected with him, we are free from the law and from control of the old sinful nature, thereby setting us free to be married to another, who is Jesus, our new husband and our new life.

All believers make up the church, and the church is the virgin bride of Christ, becoming one with him just like in a natural marriage when man and wife become one when they marry.

- We have a new Lord.

Most people who profess to be Christians do not understand the full meaning of the word *Lord* as it is used in the scriptures. A good working definition is that *Lord* means "supreme authority." We see that in the headship of Jesus over the church, which is his body, and also as the head of the wife in his marriage to the church.

In our natural body, the head always has authority over our hands, fingers, arms, legs, feet, and so on; likewise, Jesus is Lord and has authority over his body; which is the church that is made up of all true believers.

When asking professing Christians the question, "do you want a savior?" all of them will say yes but asked if they want a Lord to have total authority over them, most people hesitate a little because our old human nature likes to be in charge, to call the shots. Our flesh does not like God's word! God's word is in direct opposition with our old desires, which are the lust of the eye, the lust of the flesh, and the pride of life.

There is a battle royal raging inside us constantly to have control over our bodies, our minds, our wills, and our emotions; and we have the choice to obey the Holy Spirit or to obey the flesh.

> What? Know ye not that your body is the temple of the Holy Ghost which is in you, which ye have of God, and ye are not your own? For ye are bought with a price; therefore glorify God in your body, and in your spirit, which are God's. (1 Corinthians 6:19–20)

> That if thou shalt confess with the mouth the Lord Jesus, and shalt believe in thine heart that God hath raised him from the dead, thou shalt be saved. For whosoever shall call upon the name of the Lord shall be saved. (Romans 10:9, 13)

Jesus is both Lord and Savior, but we have to recognize him as the *supreme authority* in both roles to be in God's will.

God the Father tells us about the power and authority that he has given to Jesus in the following scriptures:

> Which he wrought in Christ, when he raised him from the dead, and set him at his own right hand in the heavenly places, far above all principality,

and power, and might, and dominion, and every name that is named, not only in this world, but also in that which is to come; and hath put all things under his feet, and gave him to be the head over all things to the church, which is his body, the fullness of him that filleth all in all. (Ephesians 1:20–23)

And why call ye me Lord, Lord and do not the things which I say? (Luke 6:46)

The remedy to restore our fellowship is to humble ourselves and confess our lack of obedience as sin so that we may be back in a righteous standing before God.

If we confess our sins, he is faithful and just to forgive us our sins, and to cleanse us from all unrighteousness. (1 John 1:9)

After confessing our sins and being cleansed, we are fit to come into God's presence through Jesus Christ our Lord to worship, to study, and to offer up prayers.

God makes available to us all things, and they are free, and they are all new to us when we are newborn babies in Christ. But as we grow and grow, we will experience more new things that God provides for us when we feed on his word. We cannot find the end of his blessings; they just keep coming and coming, more and more, better and better. Praise the Lord for them all.

JESUS CHRIST, OUR ALL IN ALL

Jesus is the Creator of all things and the Communicator in the scriptures.

Contrary to most churchgoer's opinion that God the Father was the Creator in Genesis chapter 1, the scriptures tell a different story, which you will see in the following scriptures:

> In the beginning was the word, and the word was with God, *and the word was God.* The same was in the beginning with God. *All things were made by him; and without him was not any thing made that was made. And the word was made flesh, and dwelt among us,* (and we beheld his glory, the glory as of the only begotten of the Father,) full of grace and truth. (John 1:1–3,14, emphasis mine)

> And to make all men see what is the fellowship of the mystery, which from the beginning of the world hath been hid in God, *who created all things by Jesus Christ.* (Ephesians 3:9, emphasis mine)

> God who at sundry times and in divers manners spake in time past unto the fathers by the prophets, hath in these last days spoken to us by his Son, whom he hath appointed heir of all things,

by whom also he made the worlds. (Hebrews 1:1–
2, emphasis mine)

*By the word of the Lord were the heavens made; and
all the host of them* by the breath of his mouth, for
he spake, and it was done; he commanded and it
stood fast. (Psalm 33:6, 9, emphasis mine)

In whom [Jesus] we have redemption through
his blood, even the forgiveness of sins; *who is the
image of the invisible God,* the firstborn of every
creature: *For by him were all things created, that
are in heaven, and that are in earth, visible and
invisible, whether they be thrones, or dominions, or
principalities, or powers: All things were created by
him, and for him: And he is before all things, and
by him all things consist.* And he is the head of
the body, the church; who is the beginning, *the
firstborn from the dead: that in all things he might
have the preeminence* [first place]. (Colossians
1:14–18)

Jesus is the Word in the Old Testament as well as in the New
Testament. And when the scriptures say *Jehovah* or *Lord,* they are
talking about Jesus Christ, the King of kings and Lord of lords.

These [gentile powers] shall make war with the
Lamb, and the Lamb shall overcome them; for he
is Lord of lords, and King of kings: and they that
are with him are called, and chosen, and faithful
[believers]. (Revelation 17:14)

And he hath on his vesture and on his thigh a
name written, King of kings and Lord of lords [at
Jesus's second coming]. (Revelation 19:16)

For in him [Jesus] dwelleth all the fullness of the
Godhead bodily [meaning that, when we look at
Jesus, we see God the Father, God the Son, and
God the Holy Spirit]. (Colossians 2:9)

In the Old Testament, Jesus appeared many, many times and
spoke to the prophets and others. And in the New Testament, he
humbled himself and took on a robe of flesh to present himself
indeed the Savior of the whole world and also to set an example for
us, to show us the Father, and to give us instruction on righteous
living, plus lots of other wonderful benefits.

Impossible, you say? Creator and Communicator?

Then came the word of the Lord unto Jeremiah,
saying, Behold, *I am the Lord, the God of all
flesh: Is there any thing too hard for me?* (Jeremiah
32:26–27, emphasis mine)

Any spiritual knowledge, access to God the Father, blessings in
this life as well as in eternity—we get all things through Jesus our
Lord. *He is God's all in all for us, the Creator and also the Communicator.*

Jesus is the I AM in the scriptures.

In Exodus chapter 3, when Moses saw the burning bush that
was not consumed, he turned aside to see why it was not burnt, and
the Lord saw him turn aside and called out from the bush and said,
"Moses, Moses," and Moses said, "Here am I," and the Lord said, "Put
off your shoes for you are on holy ground." God also told Moses that
he was the God of his ancestors, and he had come down to deliver
his people from their oppressors in Egypt, and he told Moses that he
would send him to lead his people out to a land flowing with milk and
honey and that he would certainly be *with him* in this journey.

And Moses said unto God, behold, when I come
unto the children of Israel, and shall say unto

them, the God of your fathers hath sent me unto you; and they shall say to me, what is his name? What shall I say unto them? And God said unto him, I AM THAT I AM: and he said, thus shalt thou say unto the children of Israel, *I AM hath sent me unto you.* And God said moreover unto Moses, thus shalt thou say unto the children of Israel, the Lord God of your fathers, the God of Abraham, the God of Isaac, and the God of Jacob, hath sent me unto you: this my name for ever, and this my memorial unto all generations. (Exodus 3:13–15, emphasis mine)

Jesus is the I AM in the Old Testament as well as in the New Testament and claims to be him seven times in the gospel of John.

I am the living bread which came down from heaven: if any man eat of this bread, he shall live forever: and the bread that I will give him is my flesh, which I will give for the life of the world. (John 6:51, emphasis mine)

Then spoke Jesus again unto them, saying, *I am the light of the world*: he that followeth me shall not walk in darkness, but shall have the light of life. (John 8:12, emphasis mine)

Then said Jesus unto them again, verily, verily I say unto you, *I am the door of the sheep.* (John 10:7, emphasis mine)

I Am the good shepherd: the good shepherd giveth his life for the sheep (John 10:11, emphasis mine)

Jesus said unto her, *I am the resurrection, and the life*: he that believeth in me, though he were dead, yet shall he live. (John 11:25, emphasis mine)

Jesus said unto him *I am the way, the truth, and the life*: no man cometh unto the Father, but by me. (John 14:6, emphasis mine)

I am the vine, ye are the branches: he that abideth in me, and I in him, the same bringeth forth much fruit: for without me ye can do nothing. (John 15:5, emphasis mine)

Jesus, when talking to the Pharisees in John 8:58, said unto them, "Verily, verily, I say unto you, *before Abraham was I am.*"

Jesus has always been; he is now and is everlasting, and all believers are in him. Knowing this should bring lots of comfort, joy, and peace, to your minds and soul.

Jesus is the righteous judge of all mankind.

For as the Father raiseth up the dead, and quickeneth them; even so the Son quickeneth whom he will. For the Father judgeth no man, *but hath committed all judgement unto the Son.* (John 5:21–22, emphasis mine)

Marvel not at this: for the hour is coming, in the which all that are in the graves shall hear his voice, and shall come forth: they that have done good, unto the resurrection of life; and they that have done evil, unto the resurrection of damnation. (John 5:28–29)

I charge thee therefore before God, and *the Lord Jesus Christ, who shall judge the quick and the dead*

> at his appearing and his kingdom. (2 Timothy
> 4:1, emphasis mine)

> And as it is appointed unto men once to die, but
> after this the judgment. (Hebrews 9:27)

We do not get God's judgment in this life, but we do get chastisement and loss of joy, peace, fellowship, and the loss of a clear conscience toward God when we disobey and don't confess our sins for cleansing from all unrighteousness. Also, after humbling ourselves and confessing our sins, we still suffer the lingering consequences of the sinful actions that we have committed. But we can have confidence that we are back in fellowship with God because God always forgives a broken heart and a contrite spirit. God is in the forgiving business; that is his love in action to us.

> If we confess our sins, he is faithful and just to
> forgive us our sins, and to cleanse us from all
> unrighteousness. (1 John 1:9)

There are two judgments that we want to mention.

First, the judgment seat of Christ, where all believers will be judged, not for sins that we have committed because all of them—past, present, and future—have been paid for by Jesus's sacrificial death, burial, and resurrection, making way for the free gift of salvation for all who will believe that his righteous, sinless blood washed away their sins and also the sins of all mankind.

> For we [believers] must all appear before the
> judgment seat of Christ; that every one may
> receive the things done in his body, according to
> that he hath done, whether it be good or bad. (2
> Corinthians 5:10)

Only the true children of God will be there and will be judged for works (service) to receive rewards or to suffer loss.

The Apostle Paul, writing to believers in Corinth, explains this judgment.

> Now if any man build on this foundation [Jesus] gold, silver, precious stones, wood, hay, stubble; every man's work shall be made manifest; for the day shall declare it, because it shall be revealed by fire; and the fire shall try every man's work of what sort it is. If any man's work abide which he hath built thereupon, he shall receive a reward. If any man's work shall be burned, he shall suffer loss: but he himself shall be saved; yet so as by fire. (1 Corinthians 3:12–15)

Good work equals service done in the spirit, attitude, love, and the same motivation that Jesus showed us and said, "follow me."

Bad works equal things that are done to satisfy our ego, for popularity, to follow the crowd, to exalt man and his programs that are not according to the scriptures, anything not showing forth the fruit of the Holy Spirit in our lives. All the bad works will be for naught and will be burned up and will bring shame.

Second: The great white throne judgment, where only lost people (the unsaved) will be there, the people who did not have faith in Christ and his finished work on the cross, thereby nullifying for themselves *the free gift of salvation that is extended to all mankind.*

> And I saw the dead [unbelievers], small and great, stand before God; and the books were opened: and another book was opened, which is the book of life: and the dead were judged out of those things which were written in the books, according to their works. And the sea gave up the dead which were in it; and death and hell delivered up the dead which were in them: and they were judged every man according to their works. And death and hell were cast into the lake of fire. This

the second death. And whosoever was not found written in the book of life was cast into the lake of fire. (Revelation 20:12–15)

These people were not judged for their sins for salvation purposes; they were being judged to determine their degree of everlasting punishment according to their evil deeds. All their sins were paid for on the cross just like everyone else, but they did not have the faith to be overcomers and had their names blotted out of the Book of Life.

> *He that overcometh*, the same shall be clothed in white raiment: [signifying righteousness] and *I will not blot out his name out of the book of life*, but I will confess his name before my Father, and before his angels; (Revelation 3:5, emphasis mine)

Who then is the overcomer? That answer is found in the following scripture:

> For whatsoever is born of God overcometh the world: and this is the victory that overcometh the world, even *our faith*. (1 John 5:4, emphasis mine)

Faith is the only thing that determines salvation; all mankind's deeds and his works are for rewards (good) in heaven or his degree of punishment (evil deeds of the lost) in the lake of fire.

Jesus's judgment is always righteous; he does not make any mistakes in judging or anything else. And all heaven will praise him for it!

Jesus is our example to live by.

In the garden of Eden, Adam and Eve ate of the tree of the knowledge of good and evil that God commanded them not to eat.

> And the Lord God commanded the man, saying, of every tree of the garden thou mayest freely

eat: but of the tree of the knowledge of good and evil, thou shalt not eat of it: for in the day that thou eatest thereof thou shalt surely die. (Genesis 2:16–17)

The very day that they ate the forbidden fruit, they surely died spiritually (separated from God) and began suffering the curses that God initiated because of their disobedience.

And the Lord God said, behold, *the man is become as one of us, to know good and evil*: and now, lest he put forth his hand, and take also of the tree of life, and eat, and live for ever: therefore the Lord God sent him forth from the garden of Eden, to till the ground from whence he was taken. (Genesis 3:22–23, emphasis mine)

Adam shows forth faith in Genesis 3:20, "And Adam called his wife's name Eve; because she was the mother of all living," and God responded in Genesis 3:21, "Unto Adam and also to his wife did the Lord God make coats of skins, and clothed them."

This clothing signified righteousness (to hide their sin: disobedience), and Adam and Eve were once more in fellowship with God. But, they were not innocent as before their disobedience. They now knew the difference between good and evil, and thus, they had a conscience. From that point forward, the example to live by was to do good, pleasing God, obeying his word, and not evil (anything that doesn't please God: sin) *so as to maintain a clear conscience toward God.*

We can see this at work in Cain and Abel's sacrifices; both knew what God desired (a blood sacrifice), but Cain would not humble himself to please God and only wanted to please himself by bringing his own works (self-righteousness) and was rejected by God. Abel brought a blood sacrifice, therefore, pleasing God and was accepted by him, giving Abel a clear conscience toward God; and he was in fellowship with him.

Even today, all mankind has the conscience to know good from evil.

> For the grace of God that bringeth salvation hath appeared to all men, teaching us that denying ungodliness and worldly lusts, we should live soberly, righteously, and godly, in this present world. (Titus 2:11–12)

So man's example to live by was a clear conscience toward God in all things revealed to him by God's Word and was attained by obedience to his instruction.

> And God saw that the wickedness of man was great in the earth, and that every imagination of the thoughts of his heart was only evil continually. (Genesis 6:5)

Mankind failed miserably, and God brought judgment on them with the flood. And after that, all men were under their consciences until God called out a peculiar people through Abraham, Isaac, and Jacob's bloodline to be separated unto himself and gave them (Israel) a new set of laws (the ten commandments) to live by, which God gave to Moses to give unto the children of Israel for them to obey in order to keep a clear conscience toward God. The law was a higher standard, a closer relationship, more detailed for God's chosen people to obey and to set an example for the Gentiles. Moses's message from God to the Israelites was in the following scripture:

> Now therefore, *if ye will obey my voice indeed, and keep my covenant, then ye shall be a peculiar treasure unto me above all people: for all the earth is mine*: and ye shall be unto me *a kingdom of priests, and an holy nation.* These are the words which thou shalt speak unto the children of Israel. And Moses came out and called for the

elders of the people, and laid before their faces all these words which the Lord commanded him. *And all the people answered together, and said, All that the Lord hath spoken we will do.* And Moses returned the words of the people unto the Lord. (Exodus 19:5–8, emphasis mine)

The Israelites failed to keep the commandments of God (the law), *which was their example to live by to have a clear conscience toward God.* But God, in his love, mercy, and his grace, sent his Son, Jesus, to fulfill the law, bringing an end to it and blotting it out through his sacrificial death, burial, and his resurrection from the dead, thereby paying the sin price for all mankind's sins for the past, present, and his future sins for salvation purposes (to be saved).

Israel, when they fell short of obeying the law (their example to live by), had to bring a proper blood sacrifice to the priest, and then he would perform the sacrificial offering according to God's ordinances so that their sins would be covered, giving the sinner a clear conscience toward God and being back in fellowship with him.

While *the Israelites were under the law,* which was their measuring stick to live up to, *the Gentiles remained under their conscience of good and evil* to live up to. But today, we (the Israelites and Gentiles) are in the same boat, as we see in the following scripture:

Wherefore remember, that ye being in time past Gentiles in the flesh, who are called uncircumcision by that which is called the circumcision in the flesh made by hands; that at that time *ye were without Christ, being aliens from the commonwealth of Israel, and strangers from the covenants of promise, having no hope, and without God in the world; But now in Christ Jesus ye who sometimes were far off are made nigh by the blood of Christ.* For he is our peace, who hath made both one, and hath broken down the middle wall of partition between us; *having abolished in his flesh the*

*enmity, even the law of commandments contained
in ordinances [Moses's law); for to make in himself
twain [Jew and Gentile] one new man,* so making
peace; and that he might reconcile *both unto God
in one body [the church]* by the cross, having slain
the enmity thereby: For through him we both
have access by one Spirit unto the Father. Now
therefore ye are no more strangers and foreign-
ers, but fellow citizens with the saints, and of the
household of God. (Ephesians 2:11–19, emphasis mine)

Since there is no longer the law (Jesus fulfilled it) for a measuring stick (example) to live up to in this age of grace, what or who do
we measure ourselves by to be pleasing to God the Father?

Remember that mankind is in a progressive relationship that
elevates him from one level of glory to another level of glory according to God's revelation of himself to man, and that relationship rises
higher and higher, more intimate and more intimate if man believes
God's Word and obeys it, making the believer more and more like
Jesus.

For all have sinned and come short of the glory of
God (did not measure up). (Romans 3:23)

God's glory being what? The Bible tells us plainly in these
scriptures.

God who at sundry times and in divers manners
spoke in times past unto the fathers by the prophets, hath in these last days spoken unto us by his
Son, whom he hath appointed heir of all things,
by whom also he made the worlds; *who being the
brightness of his glory, and the express image of his
person,* and upholding all things by the word of
his power, when he had by himself purged our

sins, sat down on the right hand of the majesty on high. (Hebrews 1:1–3, emphasis mine)

For God, who commanded the light shine out of darkness, hath shined in our hearts, to give *the light of the knowledge of the glory of God in the face of Jesus Christ*. (2 Corinthians 4:6, emphasis mine)

Folks, *when we see Jesus, we see the glory of God*; therefore, Jesus Christ, our Lord, is who we measure ourselves by in this age of grace. *He is our example* to follow in all things.

For this is thankworthy, if a man *for conscience toward God* endure grief, suffering wrongfully. For what glory is it, if, when ye be buffeted for your faults, ye take it patiently? But if, when ye do well, and suffer for it, ye take it patiently, this is acceptable with God. *For even hereunto were ye called: because Christ also suffered for us, leaving us an example [to live up to], that ye should follow his steps*: Who did no sin, neither was guile found in his mouth: Who, when he was reviled, reviled not again; when he suffered, he threatened not; but committed himself to him that judgeth righteously: (1 Peter 2:19–23, emphasis mine)

If we don't measure up to *Jesus who is the glory of God*, how do we get our prayers answered? How do we get a clear conscience toward God? How do we get righteous enough to enter into his presence? For all have come short of Jesus's examples in words, deeds, thoughts, and motives, and not humbling ourselves before God. We find the answers to these questions in God's word.

If we confess our sins, he is faithful and just to forgive us our sins, and to cleanse us from all unrighteousness. (1 John 1:9)

If we have no unrighteousness, then we are perfect in God's eyes just like Jesus and can fellowship with God, come to his table and feed on his word, have our prayers answered, and have a clear conscience toward God. We have humbled ourselves, confessed our sins, which is to be like Jesus was when he humbled himself and went to the cross for us.

> Let this mind be in you, which was also in Christ Jesus: Who being in the form of God, thought it not robbery to be equal with God. But made himself of no reputation, and took upon him the form of a servant, and was made in the likeness of men: And being found in fashion as a man, he humbled himself and became obedient unto death, even the death of the cross. (Philippians 2:5–8)

> The Lord is nigh unto them that are of a broken heart, and saveth such as be of a contrite spirit. (Psalm 34:18)

> The sacrifices of God are a broken spirit; a broken and contrite heart, o God, thou wilt not despise. (Psalm 51:17)

> For thus saith the high and lofty one that inhabiteth eternity, whose name is Holy; I dwell in the high and holy place, with him also that is of a contrite and humble spirit, to revive the heart of the contrite ones. (Isaiah 57:15)

> Thus saith the Lord, the heaven is my throne, and the earth is my footstool: Where is the house that ye build unto me? And where is the place of my rest? For all those things hath mine hand made, and all those things have been, saith the

Lord; but to this man will I look, even to him that is poor and of a contrite spirit, and trembleth at my word. (Isaiah 66:1–2)

These people who are of a broken heart and a contrite spirit (humble and confessing their sins) are the only ones whom God will fellowship with because he demands absolute perfection in his presence, which we have through our being in Christ and confessing our sins.

We are the body of Christ; he is the head. He is our example in all facets of our lives!

For *Christ is the end of the law for righteousness* to everyone that believeth. (Romans 10:4, emphasis mine)

The law was fulfilled and ended on the cross by Jesus Christ, and the believer is on a higher calling than Israel, and we more than fulfill the law when we act out of love in all things like Jesus, our example, did. Also, our consciences are clear toward God, as we love him and all others.

For all the law is fulfilled in one word, even in this; Thou shalt love thy neighbor as thyself. (Galatians 5:14)

Jesus is our soul rest.

Soul rest is the state that our minds, wills, and emotions long for, which is a promise for believers that Jesus gave in the following scriptures:

Come unto me, all ye that labour and are heavy laden, and I will give you rest [that was for salvation and to have *peace with God*]. Take my yoke upon you, and learn of me; for I am meek and lowly in heart; and ye shall find rest unto your souls [this is for worship, service, and for fellowship, and also to have the *peace of God* in us; that we may live the abundant life]. (Matthew 11:28–29)

The thief cometh not, but for to steal, and to kill, and to destroy: I am come that they might have life, and that they might have it more abundantly. (John 10:10)

We will get a clearer understanding of our promise of soul rest when we compare it with the promise given to Israel on their journey to the promised land, which was the earthly rest for God's earthly people.

Indeed, Israel had been saved from Egypt (a symbol of sin in scripture) and were God's chosen people, and had seen miracles and mighty works that God had done on their behalf and were promised that his angel would lead them unto a land flowing with milk and honey and give them houses, crops, vineyards, and cities that they did not have to build or work for. He also promised good health and prosperity if they would obey his commandments. We find more promises in the following scripture:

There shall nothing cast their young, nor be barren, in thy land: the number of thy days I will fulfil. I will send my fear before thee, and will destroy all the people to whom thou shall come, and I will make all thine enemies turn their backs unto thee. And *I will send hornets before thee, which shall drive out the Hivite, the Canaanite, and the Hittite,* from before thee. I will not drive them out from before thee in one year; lest the land become desolate, and the beast of the field multiply against thee. By *little and little I will drive them out* from before thee, until thou

be increased, and inherit the land [their rest].
(Exodus 23:26–30, emphasis mine)

Israel did not believe that God would drive out their enemies
by the hornets and wanted to send in spies to scout out the promised
land. God allowed them to send in the spies (he does not force his
people to obey his word, but they will suffer the consequences of
their actions and attitudes). After the return of the spies, they made
their assessment and decided that they could not win the battles over
their enemies. They were relying on their own ideas and might for
the victory, not God's provisions.

That disobedience caused the Israelites to wander around in the
wilderness for forty years until all the faithless men twenty years old
and older died out except Joshua and Caleb who listened to God but
couldn't persuade the others to obey.

We have an account of God's reply concerning their lack of
faith in the book of Hebrews.

> But with whom was he grieved forty years? Was
> it not with them that had sinned, whose carcases
> fell in the wilderness? And to whom sware he that
> they should not enter into his rest, but to them
> that believed not? *So we see that they could not
> enter in because of unbelief.* (Hebrews 3:17–19,
> emphasis mine)

The true saints of today have a promise of rest but not an earthly
and materialistic rest. Unlike what God's chosen people were promised
in the Old Testament, our rest is a spiritual rest (soul rest) for God's
heavenly people to enjoy regardless of the circumstances and the predic-
aments that we find ourselves experiencing in this world. Because Jesus
told us in John 17:16: "They are not of this world, even as I am not of
this world" (he was talking to his disciples and included us in verse 20).

> Blessed be the God and Father of our Lord Jesus
> Christ, which according to his abundant mercy,

hath begotten us again unto a lively hope by the resurrection of Jesus Christ from the dead, *to an inheritance incorruptible, and undefiled, and that fadeth not away, reserved in heaven for you, who are kept by the power of God through faith unto salvation* ready to be revealed in the last time. (1 Peter 1:3–5, emphasis mine)

Through faith we are saved, and that gives us peace with God.

> *For by grace are ye saved through faith*: and that not of yourselves; *it is the gift of God: Not of works*, lest any man should boast. (Ephesians 2:8–9, emphasis mine)

After salvation, the soul rest that all of us long for is the very *peace of God*, and we get the formula for that from the following scripture:

> Take my yoke [not yours or mine but Jesus's yoke] upon you, and learn of me; for I am meek and lowly in heart: and ye shall find rest unto your souls. (Matthew 11:29)

You may ask, What was Jesus's yoke? The Bible tells us in these scriptures.

> Wherefore when he cometh into the world, he saith, Sacrifice and offering thou wouldest not, but *a body thou hast prepared me*: In burnt-offerings and sacrifices for sin thou hast had no pleasure. Then said I, *lo, I come* [in the volume of the book it is written of me] *to do thy will o God*. (Hebrews 10:5–7, emphasis mine)

Above when he said, Sacrifice and offering and burnt-offerings and offering for sin thou wouldest not, neither hadst pleasure therein; which are offered by the law; Then said he, lo, *I come to do thy will o God*. He taketh away the first, [the law] that he may establish the second [grace]. *By the which will we are sanctified through the offering of the body of Jesus Christ once for all.* (Hebrews 10:8–10, emphasis mine)

I can of mine own self do nothing: As I Hear I judge: and my judgment is just; because I seek not mine own will, but the will of the Father which hath sent me. (John 5:30)

For I came down from heaven, not to do mine own will, but the will of him that sent me. (John 6:38)

And he that sent me is with me: the Father hath not left me alone; *for I do always those things that please him*. (John 8:29, emphasis mine)

Jesus's yoke was to always do the will of the Father in all things. That same yoke is the one that we are to take upon ourselves, but he didn't stop there. He also said *learn of me*; it is after learning of Jesus (the position that we have in him, plus his advocate work as our high priest, plus all the new things available to us, and the Holy Spirit's work, and His power, and all God's other benefits that are freely given to us) that we know that God is in control of all things, that he is sovereign and does all things after the counsel of his own will; and no one can stop him. But the best thing that comforts us having soul rest is that God rules, overrules, and universally rules everything, and all things that God has, we will share with Jesus and that God the Father, God the Son, and God the Holy Spirit make their home in us, the believer.

When God drove the enemies of Israel out of the promised land, he didn't drive them out all at once, but he said little by little. And this is a lesson for us because when we are saved, it is an instantaneous and a one-time experience; that is, the rest mentioned in Matthew 11:28, *which is for peace with God* (salvation). Matthew 11:29 is for sanctification, which is for worship, service, fellowship, to have a clear conscience toward God, and for intimacy with God and Jesus: *this is the peace of God (soul rest).*

We are babes in Christ at the born-again experience, then we feed on milk and progress little by little toward adulthood by feasting on God's word and obeying it for a clear conscience toward God. Israel progressed toward their *earthly rest* little by little, and God's heavenly people (the church) progress toward our *soul rest* little by little.

> Till we all come in the unity of the faith, and of the knowledge of the Son of God, unto a perfect [mature] man, *unto the measure of the stature of the fullness of Christ* [until we become just like Christ By taking his yoke upon us]. (Ephesians 4:13, emphasis mine)

> My little children, of whom I travail in birth again *until Christ be formed in you.* (Galatians 4:19, emphasis mine)

So we see then this soul rest is attained through faith and the knowledge and obedience to God's word as we see in the following scripture:

> But without faith it is impossible to please him: for he that cometh to God must believe that he is and that *he is a rewarder of them that diligently seek him.* (Hebrews 11:6, emphasis mine)

Let us look back and see how Israel finally entered into their rest.

> And ye went over Jordan, and came unto Jericho: And the men of Jericho fought against you, the Amorites, and the Perizzites, and the Canaanites, and the Hittites, and the Girgashites, the Hivites, and the Jebusites; and I delivered them into your hand. *And I sent the hornet before you, which drove them out before you*, even the two kings of the Amorites; but not with thy sword, nor with thy bow [not with human strength or weapons]. And I have given you a land for which ye did not labor, and cities which ye built not, and ye dwell in them; of the vineyards and olive yards which ye planted not do ye eat. Now therefore fear the Lord, and serve him in sincerity and truth. (Joshua 24:11–14, emphasis mine)

Israel entered the promised land (their rest) by God's provision, *the hornet*, just as he said that he would do forty years earlier. They didn't believe him then, so they couldn't receive their rest. And so it is today for each and every believer.

> Trust in the Lord with all thine heart; and lean not unto thine own understanding. In all thy ways acknowledge him, and he shall direct thy paths. Be not wise in thine own eyes: fear the Lord and depart from evil. (Proverbs 3:5–7)

> Wherefore be ye not unwise, but understanding what the will of the Lord is. (Ephesians 5:17)

In these times of troubles, trials and tribulation, social unrest, and a worldwide pandemic, every Christian needs to have the soul rest that Jesus gives to keep them steady and on course toward maturity in Christ and to be the witness that God desires of us.

Jesus himself gives us an example of what it is like to have soul rest by his work on the cross, saying, "Father, into thy hands I commend my spirit," (Luke 23:46) fully trusting in the Father's will as we should. And in another place, another example:

> For this is thankworthy, if a man for conscience toward God endure grief, suffering wrongfully. For what glory is it, if, when ye be buffeted for your faults, ye shall take it patiently? This is acceptable with God. For even hereunto were ye called: because *Christ also suffered for us, leaving us an example that ye should follow his steps*: who did no sin, neither was guile found in his mouth: Who, when he was reviled, reviled not again; when he suffered, he threatened not; but committed himself to him that judgeth righteously [wanted the Father's will to be done]. (1 Peter 2:19–23, emphasis mine)

Everything that we see around us today in our families, our government, and in our churches, and the rest of the world paints a bleak and discouraging picture. But remember, God is still in control of all things, and all these things that we see have to come to pass before the rapture takes place and for the Antichrist to be revealed and for Jesus to return to set up his earthly kingdom.

Neither politicians, kings, nor mankind will solve our problems; they will become more and more complex. Only God has the answers to all our problems and the world's problems. But we can have soul rest by humbling ourselves and abiding in Christ, staying in fellowship with the Father, and by walking in the Spirit as we are challenged to do in the scriptures, and all these by the power given to us by the Holy Spirit. As we do these things, we will fulfill these next two scriptures.

And whatsoever ye do in word or deed; do all in
the name of the Lord Jesus, giving thanks to God
and the Father by him. And whatsoever ye do, do
it heartily, as unto the Lord, and not unto men.
(Colossians 3:17, 23)

Ye are the light of the world. A city that is set on
a hill cannot be hid. (Matthew 5:14)

Our prayer is that God will bless you and give you grace for
your ministry of reconciliation as you grow toward soul rest and
maturity in Christ.

ABOUT THE AUTHOR

Glenn is an eighty-two-year-old believer married to Sarah, his wife of fifty-seven years, with three children and seven grandsons. Glenn has been a Sunday school teacher almost thirty years and has one other work published—*All Prisoners Can Be Free*.

He is active in Sulphur Springs Baptist Church of Pilot Mountain, North Carolina, and is an avid Bible student.

CPSIA information can be obtained
at www.ICGtesting.com
Printed in the USA
JSHW022139300622
27468JS00007B/16